For my teacher, Don J

With this book may the me............... me ...naman, Ayahuasca and Mother Earth be spread far and wide and the purpose of my journey be fulfilled.

I dedicate this book to all those who are choosing love instead of fear, unity instead of separation, power instead of force and those who are walking the path of personal responsibility and conscious evolution.

*The breeze at dawn has secrets to tell you.*
*Don't go back to sleep.*
*You must ask for what you really want.*
*Don't go back to sleep.*
*People are going back and forth across the doorsill*
*Where the worlds touch.*
*The door is round and open.*
*Don't go back to sleep.*

– Jalal al-Din Rumi
*(Translated by John Moyne and Coleman Barks)*

For more information please visit
**www.theshamanslastapprentice.com**

All the experiences and events in this book are true.
Wherever possible individuals have given permission to be
named. However, this was not always possible and in those
cases names have been changed to protect their identity.

© Rebekita, 2004

Rebekita asserts the moral right to be identified as the
author of this work

A catalogue for this book is available from the
British Library

ISBN 1-904881-01-7

Summertime publishing in association with Amaru

Printed and bound in Great Britain by
Biddles Ltd
Rollesby Road, Hardwick Industrial Estate,
King's Lynn, Norfolk

Cover photograph by Michael Thornton,
www.zodiacpark.com

All rights reserved. No part of this publication may be
reproduced, stored in a retrieval system or transmitted, in
any form or by any means, electronic, mechanical,
photocopying, recording or otherwise, without the prior
permission of the publishers.

This book was printed on recycled paper

# CONTENTS

# ACKNOWLEDGEMENTS

I would first like to thank the Cosmic Universe, Mother Earth and Ayahuasca, for awakening me to who I truly am and reminding me that I am not alone – not ever. Thank you for always being a guiding light even during my darkest moments of doubt and for the love, light and blessings that are flowing down.

Thank you to my family for their support and love for my journey. My mother for showing me what I needed to see in order to be free and giving me the independence to follow my dreams, my father for guiding me on the path and for imparting the belief that nothing is impossible and my brother and sister for sharing this lifetime together.

A special thank you to Ben Rayner, my lover, soulmate and best friend for all your editing, support, hugs and love, the book would not have been the same without you.

A special thank you to Brian Kirkland for his generosity of spirit, without you the book would not have been realised.

Thank you to Peter and Ruth Terry for your wonderful hospitality and for providing me with the space and solitude to get out of my own way and allow the book to write itself.

Thank you to Ian Young for your courage, inspiration and dedication to help people overcome their addictions.

Thank you to Harry Hoelder for your unconditional love and for sharing such an important part of my life with me.

A big thank you to Michael Thornton for the front cover photograph and your friendship, love and encouragement; to Antonia Gross for proof reading the manuscript, Jo Parfitt for your advice; Sheena Jordan for typesetting and design; Babi for your unconditional love and the logo design; Amy for your love and graphic designing and Emmanuel and Michael from Neamtech who stayed up till the early hours to allow us to finish working on the book.

Thanks to Jon Baldock for editing the first draft, and to Elisabet Satoris, Jo Bloom, David Bloom, Greg Collins, Demetris Grey, Danny Simmonds, Carol Polsky, Ivor and Lesley-Jane Spector, Nikki Runyon, Pippa Vine, Anthony Patete, Sian Sullivan, Tamsin Bradley, Jon Sheaf and Toby Sturmer for all your helpful comments and suggestions.

Thanks to all my soul sisters and brothers, new and old, for your deep friendships and for following your truth – you know who you are. I would also like to thank David McCready and Erika for giving me the space to rewrite and edit the book in a creative environment.

Lastly, thank you to Paradox and all the beautiful poets, artists and musicians who are using the spoken word and creative arts to spread the message of love and change. Your passion is an inspiration to all that hear you.

I would also like to acknowledge all the wonderful people who looked after me while I was in Peru and who helped to show me the way. I have been blessed to meet some wonderful people this lifetime and I thank all those who have come into my life and enriched it with their presence.

# FOREWORD

Sometimes events unfold in a way that seems quite natural and logical afterwards but can be quite bewildering at the time. So it was with my first encounter with Rebecca. It was during an evening of song and spirituality in London in the spring of 2004 that I struck up a conversation with the vibrant young woman who had been sitting next to me. She told me that she had been writing a book. It was about her experiences during the time she spent as an apprentice to a shaman in the Amazon rainforest. Certainly a rather different way of life to the world of finance in which I worked, and a very different environment to the noise and dirt of the London streets, which awaited us outside! I was intrigued and expressed my interest in reading her story when it became available.

As Rebecca began to tell me more about the time and energy she had devoted to completing her book, and of her plans to undertake the publishing herself, I found that her phrases were resonating in an extraordinary way that was an entirely new experience for me. I had been considering how I would want to direct my life in the time ahead, once I had reached the point where my years of paid employment had drawn to a close. Now, in describing her own situation, Rebecca was utilising, one after another, the very words and expressions with which I had been conducting my own internal dialogue. I stood there quite bemused, not knowing what was happening. I could only conclude that the Universe was prodding me to provide some assistance to her publishing project.

After offering some support, a few weeks later I found myself reading the first chapters of her work. Its impact on me was immediate. I soon had no doubt that I should help Rebecca reach a wider audience with her story. I reacted to what I was reading with a degree of emotional involvement, which I had not expected. I was moved to laugh out loud in places and to share her innermost feelings of fear or despair in others. I particularly enjoyed the atmospheric descriptions of the river and its surroundings. I was impatient to read more and to know more and, when each batch arrived, the new chapters would be rapidly devoured.

From the very beginning, in our first conversation, Rebecca stressed that all she had written was true. That shines through. Her account is written with great honesty and passion, demonstrating the intensity of her experiences, with no attempt to disguise her feelings of vulnerability in the face of life's challenges. It is one person's courageous attempt to discover and live her own truth.

I was surprised to find that many of the spiritual ideas expressed in these pages were beliefs to which I could connect immediately; many I had already adopted, although I realised that it had taken me almost twice as long as Rebecca to develop my understanding. No doubt much of her learning has come through living so close to the edge, both in the rainforest and in her earlier life.

That April meeting in London, and all that began to flow from it, helped to catalyse a firm decision for me: that I would try to give a greater emphasis to Spirit, rather than intellectually-based pursuits, in my plans for the future.

I am sure that many of those reading this inspiring book will find that it can help them to find a different perspective, and so to achieve some shift in the focus of their own lives. If you are one of those, I wish you well.

Walk in the Light, and know that the courage, strength and wisdom that you need are already yours.


*Brian Kirkland*

# INTRODUCTION

In 1997, I was given the opportunity to go to Peru to work as Cultural and Activities Manager in a hotel in Machu Picchu. Despite this being a dream of mine I had a strong foreboding feeling and decided to consult a psychic that had been recommended to me. Sitting opposite her she took my hands, looked deep into my eyes, and said in a serious voice, "Rebecca, all I can see for you, if you go to Peru, is darkness, death and destruction. I advise you not to go. If you stay in London I can see you will have a very successful career in banking."

The next day I bought my plane ticket to Peru. Darkness, death and destruction sounded a lot more fun than a career in banking. But the psychic's words came partly true and during my time in Machu Picchu my whole world collapsed. One night, when I had reached the pit of despair, and not knowing where to turn, I had a vision. A shaman from deep in the heart of the Amazon had heard my heart calling. He told me it was time to learn from him, so I followed this vision, this dream, and found my teacher in a little village nestled in a remote corner of the Amazon rainforest. There I became the Shaman's last apprentice.

What follows in these pages is the true story of my journey to the Amazon and my time with the Shaman and his family, taking the sacred medicine plant, Ayahuasca, and being initiated into the ancient wisdom of the rainforest. I did not become the Shaman's apprentice because of some amazing gifts or psychic abilities that I have. Neither was I chosen because I was special. My journey of self-discovery happened because I believed, without doubt and with all my heart, that there must be another way of living, without fear or suffering, a life where I was free. And I did not give up on this, even when it seemed impossible.

This story is also a warning from the Shaman to the West that we urgently need to change our relationship with each other, and with Mother Earth. She is a living organic being preparing for her own evolution, and unconsciously we are preparing for ours. Change is in the air as our religious, economic and political systems break down, clearing the way for new beginnings and teachings based on unconditional Love. For those who are ready to embrace the way of love, life will be a joyous journey, and those who choose to hold on to what has come before will continue to live in pain and suffering. There is no right or wrong way. Each of us has the choice to live in Fear, or to live in Love.

The time has come for the individual spirit to remember that life is just a timeless journey of separation, exploration and reunion. Myths and dogma that have kept us repressed and domesticated have controlled us for centuries. We have allowed ourselves to be ruled by others, and in so doing have given up our individual power. Collectively, we have allowed the disproportionate distribution of wealth, and the disparity between the rich and the poor to grow, and now the effects of this practice can no longer be ignored.

Only together, as one race, can we change this destructive path we are treading. Only individually, by our choices, can we move mountains and topple corrupt businesses and governments, feed everyone on this planet and distribute the necessary medication to any person who needs it. Only by our choices can we end war and make this planet a Heaven on Earth. And yet change can only occur when each one of us takes the responsibility to change ourselves first.

Now it is time to wake up and evolve consciously, to start shining our light and our love. You do not need to go to the rainforest to find your divinity. It is found when you are truly happy and at peace with yourself. It is an inner journey that is unique to each individual, a universal pilgrimage called life that we are all taking, consciously or unconsciously.

We are not helpless. We are not caged. The path of conscious evolution is open to anyone who wishes to walk it.

I wish you all Love, Peace and Blessings for your journey.

*Rebekita*

# PROLOGUE

## *The Vision*

*...the veil between my rational world and the world of magic, of other dimensions, that we as humans rarely have the honour of experiencing, had lifted. A vision appeared and from the nucleus the form of a presence filled the space where the mountains had been. Nothing tangible that I could see with my physical eyes, more a feeling, a barely perceptible outline of a person that I felt I knew on a soul level.*

*There was no sound, but from the vision I heard his voice, which seemed to boom around my brain and resonated through every cell of my body. "To find who you truly are you must let go of all your dreams and expectations and come to me. I am waiting for you. Your destiny is here in the Amazon."*

*"But why the Amazon? Surely my destiny is here in Machu Picchu," I questioned.*

*"Your time in Machu Picchu was only to prepare you. Your destiny has always been with me and now you are almost ready."*

*"Ready for what?" I thought. "What is my purpose for being in Peru?"*

*"Ready to find out who you truly are," came the reply...*

## PART ONE – SEPARATION

*"Whatever you can do,
or dream you can, begin it.
Boldness has genius,
power and magic in it."*

Goethe

# CHAPTER ONE

## *Sufferings and Explorations*

I was born into a typical middle class Jewish family in London with all the opportunities and support available to live an abundant and comfortable life. I thought I had everything I needed both materially and emotionally and for the first few years my life was pretty much a happy existence.

The first time I was aware that all was not harmonious in the world was when my father took my brother and I to see the animated film, 'Watership Down'. I was four years old and blissfully innocent. For me, life was about playing, and love, and laughter, and friendships and I didn't know what it was to fear. The film is about a group of rabbits whose warren is crushed when their field is destroyed to make room for a housing development. I was so distraught by the film that my father had to carry me out half way through, and I was plagued by nightmares for weeks afterwards at the death of the rabbits and the destruction of nature. After a similar experience with the Disney cartoon, 'Cinderella' and the cruelty of the ugly sisters to the heroine, I was banned from seeing any film that caused distress to animals or humans.

But my eyes had been opened and everywhere I looked I saw cruelty and injustice. At the age of eight I organised fundraising for starving children in Africa, and a year later I was championing the cause of the elephants murdered for their ivory. I wanted to make this world a better place – to free it from suffering so that everyone would be happy.

My father was going through a spiritual awakening of his own at this time. Having reached the pinnacle of success at a young age, he realised he had not found happiness. He had achieved all his materialistic dreams and yet the lack of fulfilment weighed heavily on his heart. He was restless and frustrated and began to explore the reasons for his dissatisfaction, despite having everything money could buy. My mother, a practical and down-to-earth woman, was not interested in asking the same questions. So he shared some of his journey with me and together we explored esoteric ideas. I became particularly interested in the concepts of karma, reincarnation and past lives, as well as meditation.

At eleven, I started at a Jewish secondary school that was a concrete jungle in the centre of London, devoid of greenery, or any nature. I used to look out of the window over a grey and desolate city and wonder what I was doing there. Our family had also run into financial problems as my father delved more into the esoteric world and rejected material life. My father had so clearly shown me that money couldn't bring happiness, and yet without it things changed for the worse in our house. My mother withdrew from the marriage, as did my father, and though there was no outward disharmony there was an underlying sense of separation and discontent. As my parents became absorbed with their own inner turmoil they became less focused on my siblings and me. We were free to do whatever we liked, and I chose to follow the world of magic and spirituality that my father was exploring. Soon I had become more and more disconnected from the 'real' world I was forced to live in by society, represented by my mother.

By the time I was thirteen years old I was tired of not knowing where I fitted in or belonged. I began to hate with a deep loathing the small-mindedness and narrow perspective of my peers. Their worries amounted to what they looked like, their weight, what boy they fancied and the latest fashion, while I was worrying about nuclear war. I became angry at what we were doing to each other and to our beautiful planet, because I did not know how to change it or help make it better. I was different, misunderstood. I felt like an outcast. Everyone else around me seemed happy to live their insular existence, disinterested in what was happening in the rest of the world and even less interested in integrating with other races or cultures. As I felt more estranged and separated from the community within which I lived it was as if I was losing everything.

I was also filled with guilt. My identity was as a Jew, and Judaism was my connection to God and to my purpose in life. I really wanted to belong, needed to belong, needed to know who I truly was. I began to blame myself for everything. Something had to be wrong with me for thinking and acting so differently and out of place for a Jewish girl.

I soon fell into the deep abyss of despair and depression. I was plagued with questions that I could not answer: Why was life such a struggle? Why is there so much hatred? Why do we hurt each other? What had happened to love? Why was I so helpless? Why was no one happy? And more and more I wondered what there was to live for. All around me my misery was reflected on the news, on television and in the newspapers. There did not seem to be any way to escape the suffering. I turned to alcohol to help numb the pain but it only fed my dark despair. Soon I began to convince myself it would be all right to die. As I saw my life loom before me, filled with this helpless isolation, I began to seriously think of committing suicide.

Then, after a particularly lonely day at school, the spark of hope that was keeping me alive died, and I felt detached and empty. It was time to leave this world and find peace and harmony. To find a place where happiness existed, where I really did belong and would be accepted for who I truly was. Death did not scare me. I just had a deep sense of resignation that left me calm and centred, relieved that I had made the decision. After crying myself empty for the grief I knew I would leave behind, but believing I had no other choice, I swallowed the few remaining pills from a bottle of paracetamol that I found in our medicine cabinet. I lay down on my bed with a mixture of fear and relief. I was giving up, but there had to be something better waiting on the other side. Hell for me was staying alive.

I found myself in a tunnel. It was long, dark and womb-like, and at the other end was a warm pulsating white light with translucent figures beckoning me. I felt a flow of love wash over me as I began to walk towards them. I was going home. I had made it to the other side. I was going to a place of peace where I would be safe and secure and never feel separated again.

I was half way to the light when I heard a noise. I turned around and saw my mother and my grandmother some way behind me. Both were crying, tears pouring out of their eyes, grief and sadness etched into their faces. My mother took a step towards me, and as she did so I felt for the first time her overwhelming love for me. Throughout my childhood my mother had found it difficult to express her love, but at that moment it consumed me. And then she spoke with the language of the heart:

*"Rebecca, your birthright as a human being is freedom of choice. The ultimate choice is the one between life and death. Your loss of identity has brought you to this point and has influenced you to choose death. But remember, before birth, as a soul, you chose life and came to this earth to fulfil your destiny here.*

*Every being has a destiny. We are all connected to this great web of life, and therefore every being on this earth is sacred and important. You have taken on the human form to carry out the promises made, before you entered this body, to the many people with whom you will come in contact in this lifetime, in order to have the choice to end your karma with them.*

*Time does not exist, for it is a human construct. Although our physical bodies disintegrate our essence cannot die. It only takes on new forms that allow us to understand different experiences in different ways. Each lifetime in a particular body has the potential to lead us closer to the Truth. And the experience of life is not the destination but the journey, the evolution of the soul. All human beings are on this journey to the Self, to enlightenment, and we are all at different stages of this journey. The people who will come and go in your life all need to meet you for their own growth, and you need to meet them for your growth. We are all connected by this one destiny - to awaken and realise our inherent divinity.*

*If you do decide to walk into the light now it is the law of nature that you must return to this earth, but your suffering will be multiplied a hundred-fold for there is no escape from destiny, no escape from karma. If you choose life you will fulfil your karma, your promise to these souls this lifetime. If you choose death you will need to return again and again for many more thousands of years.*

*The only way to be free of suffering is to find out who you truly are, and then BE it in order to be free. Rebecca, with this wisdom you must now make your decision."*

Behind my mother I saw all the souls I had promised to help this lifetime. I saw thousands of people whose lives would touch mine, and mine theirs. A smile on the train, kind words to a stranger, or something more. It did not matter. In that moment I saw the grand complexity of life and the perfection of our interactions with each other. I looked towards the warm, loving light at the end of the tunnel where I knew I would be safe and secure. And then I looked again at my mother and grandmother and felt their unconditional love. In that moment I knew there was no escape from living. I had to choose life.

I awoke in the same bed, in the same bedroom, with the empty bottle beside me. For some unexplainable reason the pills had not physically affected me, nothing had changed on the surface. But deep inside I *had* changed. I looked out of the window into the dark blanket punctured with thousands of stars and smiled with an overwhelming sense of relief, as I felt the stirrings of faith once again in my heart.

\* \* \*

I now had to find my identity, and more than anything I was a Jew, belonging to this family, this ancient bloodline that I had been born into. With my new found faith I decided that I needed to give religion another chance, and consequently, a few months after my suicide attempt I went to stay in Israel on an educational exchange. Once there I immersed myself in the religious aspects of Judaism. The devout path with its strict system of belief and commandments offered a clear path and a life full of purpose. If I kept all the laws, and had absolute faith in God, I would live a pious life. It was my purpose as a Jew.

I tried with all my heart to be the good person that the religious books and teachings told me to be, and searched for the reason for my existence in religious dogma. But no matter how hard I prayed it felt so wrong, as though I was wearing someone else's ill-fitting old clothes. This religious God never seemed to be satisfied with what I had achieved, only concentrating on my faults. Even when I was keeping the laws it was never enough. I always felt as if I were sinning. This God was insatiable.

There also seemed to be a great gulf between the teachings and messages being preached from the pulpit, and what was going on in the world around me. I felt closer to God and more at peace with myself when I was out walking in the woods near my house; wandering over Hampstead Heath, watching the change of seasons in the trees; sitting by a smooth glassy lake watching the ducks waddling and paddling around; or staring at the huge darkness of space glittering with billions of stars and galaxies. In contrast, I felt myself separated from this energy when I was in a man-made place of worship, muttering controlled prayers that did not come from my heart, to a God that I felt was judging me.

The religious teachers tried to guide me, but could only offer the solace that if I followed this path unconditionally the 'world to come' would be better. I soon realised that I was not happy being this religious person. I was much more than this identity, this religion stuck in old and worn out doctrines and limitations. I decided Judaism could not help me find myself, and despite having found my faith, I couldn't rely on religion to answer the questions I was asking. Although I no longer felt the weight of despair, I still fell into a dark abyss without the strict limitations of religion. No longer having a God to guide and protect me, I felt lost and confused, not knowing where or who to turn to.

\* \* \*

At sixteen I stayed with a friend who lived in a squat in St Albans with a gang of punks. The house was in a squalid condition. It was freezing cold, and damp, with empty beer bottles and drugs strewn all over the place, and an old black and white television continuously running the video of 'Clockwork Orange'.

We experimented with heroin, cocaine, ecstasy, speed, mushrooms and a myriad of pills. All these drugs opened different doors to perception. I saw the world differently according to which drug I was currently high on. I went through the highs and lows, the madness and the miracles. I connected to the One Love and received wonderful visions. But after a while I became aware of an underlying anger that pervaded the place. It seemed to bubble under the surface, ready to explode at any moment, as it often did.

The people living in the squat were raging against the world, victims of a system they felt they had not chosen. The alcohol and drugs only fuelled their anger. They did not want to find a solution to their predicament, they only wanted to escape this world through drugs, and blame everyone else for their suffering. I found the hate suffocating and tried to explain this to my friend, but he could not hear me. He had found a group of people that mirrored his own needs to rebel against the system, and he accepted the rage as part of the deal.

I continued to experiment with different psychedelics, soon realising that although drugs can be a short cut to understanding the universe they could not show me who I truly was. Over time all they seemed to do was exacerbate my loss of identity, and after a 'trip' I often felt vulnerable as my inadequacies were magnified, leaving me less able to cope with the general ups and downs of life.

At the age of eighteen, on failing my A-Levels and re-takes I left England in search of myself. My dream was to go to Peru – to Machu Picchu - but instead I travelled to other places, from the gurus in India, to the indigenous tribes of Brazil, from the Native American Indians to the Aboriginals in Australia. During my journeys I realised I wasn't the only one who had been asking the same questions. Humans all over the world and throughout the ages have been searching for a remedy from pain and suffering in their own unique and inspired ways, and in all cultures and religions are techniques and ways to lessen misery. However, while this was reassuring, none of the paths I explored could lead me to a clearer understanding of myself.

Three years later I returned to England.

On returning I persuaded a professor, at the School of Oriental and African Studies, to accept me as a student, and completed a degree in Study of Religions. The three-year course strengthened a more positive identity by helping me overcome the feelings of failure that I experienced when I flunked my A-levels. Soon after graduating I found a job managing an esoteric gift shop in London, selling crystals, tarot and all types of books focusing on the mind, body, and spirit. I became very interested in crystal healing, as well as understanding the art of tarot and other psychic techniques. I was surprised at the diversity of people that passed through the shop, exploring alternative ways of understanding the world.

Customers were searching for the meaning of life but just didn't know where to look. Many felt that religion and God had failed them, and no longer held legitimate answers. Instead they were turning to the 'spiritual' to find reasons for their physical and emotional pain. Working in the shop gave me the opportunity to share some of what I had learned on my travels and from my degree, and it became an island in a sea of confusion. During my time at the shop it slowly dawned on me that medicine alone couldn't heal a person. My contact with people on a daily basis desperately searching for answers opened a doorway to a clearer understanding of disease. It became apparent that a much deeper process was needed to really heal someone.

Medicine could only help to heal the physical body, but illness penetrated the whole person on all the metaphysical levels. I wondered, if I found the underlying reason for human pain and suffering, would I then find the key to healing both the physical and emotional bodies? I played with this idea for a few months, but it didn't become really clear to me until one of my regular customers came in, and without knowing it gave me the answer.

It was a gloriously sunny day, the air was warm and balmy and the birds could be heard singing in the treetops. The sunlight was streaming through our windows, and although the shop had been reasonably busy with summer trade, it was now empty. At about 11.00am, the little bell signalled the arrival of a customer and I turned to greet her. She was one of my regulars.

The moment she smiled at me I knew I would never see her again after that day. She was dying and I could see in her eyes that she had accepted the inevitable call with grace and dignity. They were dull and no longer sparkled with life. I could see that she had also lost a lot of weight, despite her flowing skirt and long Indian cotton top and I tried to hide the shock on my face. Her head was covered in a trendy scarf wrapped turban style, and although it looked elegant I knew it was covering the loss of hair from chemotherapy and radiotherapy.

This woman was accepting her fate and her death. Deep within me something stirred and I felt a huge anger well up. Why had this good woman, who had fought so valiantly and so courageously, lost the fight? Why did she need to suffer like that? Why did cancer exist? How can we heal a disease like this? In all the countries I had travelled I had explored the different indigenous healing techniques that were used by local communities. On speaking to this woman, I was reminded of my dream to go to Peru, a desire forgotten in the everyday world of work.

I had always wanted to go to Machu Picchu because of its spiritual connections. This ancient Inca site is renowned as an energy centre, and has become a pilgrimage place for people seeking answers to the age-old mysteries of life. It had been my dream to live and work right in the centre of this unusually powerful place, and learn about all aspects of myself in both practical and spiritual terms. I always believed that some of the answers could be found there.

This woman affected me on a deeply profound level, and without warning the questions that had been plaguing me for most of my life began to whirl around my mind, as I got the feeling that I was missing something important. My life had settled into a comfortable routine and I was bored. I had a safe and secure future, a good job, a potential long-term career, a partner to share it with who loved and supported me, and a close group of friends. I had achieved everything I wanted. I was twenty-six, and according to my peers it was time to get married and live happily ever after.

I began to resent going into work, the routine of socialising and the pointlessness of earning money to spend it on things I didn't need, and didn't care for. I had everything I wanted, and yet I couldn't see the point of it all. There was a whole world out there ready to be explored. Suddenly the pull to find my purpose, to find who I truly was, became very strong, like a cross-tide pulling me along, and I knew it was time to go to Peru, to follow my dream.

Yet now I was getting the message to go I was afraid. I started drinking alcohol and smoking marijuana to numb out this irritating inner voice, fighting to silence it. I began to be haunted by images of Machu Picchu. When I turned on the television, or when I bought a magazine or newspaper there always seemed to be a reference to this sacred site. It was as if everything was guiding me to go to Peru. I couldn't ignore the signs when one day, as I swerved to avoid a man stepping in front of my bike, I saw that he was wearing a Machu Picchu sweater. When Harry and I started looking for a house together the feelings of restlessness got stronger and more perplexing. The doorway was opening up for me. The woman with cancer had reminded me that life was too short to be spent in fear of the unknown, and that it was time to find the courage to follow the signs.

There were mixed reactions from family and friends when I told them of my decision. My mother and some friends were disappointed that I was taking such a risk and 'running away from reality.' My father was fully supportive of the idea and encouraged me to follow the dream. Harry was devastated but did not want to end the relationship, promising to wait for me.

Suddenly things began happening very fast. Right desire and right intention are powerful forces, and life often has a funny way of leading us to the right people at the right time. The next day I wrote to a family friend who owned a hotel in the village of Aguas Calientes, next to the site of Machu Picchu, on the chance that I could go and work there as a chalet girl. I faxed him a letter with my CV and within two days he had replied. He offered me a job as the hotel's Cultural and Activities Manager, expanding and improving the boutique, as well as being responsible for entertaining the predominantly American guests.

Magically, everything fell into place. I felt strapped to the seat of a jumbo jet and there was nothing I could do except sit tight and see where I was being led. I was leaving so much behind and yet there was so much to look forward to. I was both excited and nervous. Would all my expectations come true?

* * *

Three months later I was on the plane heading to Peru. As the plane taxied along the runway and took off, my heart leapt. I was heading into the unknown, leaving behind me the man I loved, and the safety of a life I knew. I felt like Paddington Bear heading for deepest darkest Peru, and there was no turning back. The year was ready to unfold before me, and I wondered what lay in store, what adventures I would have that would challenge and change me. Most of all I wondered whether this time I would really find what I was looking for.

## CHAPTER TWO

## *Machu Picchu*

The tropical thunderstorm raged around me as I stood on the balcony outside the small hotel office. It was a powerful display as lightening crackled and bounced around the mountaintops, and the deafening claps of thunder echoing across the valley smothered the roar of the river. The rain fell in sheets across the hotel, driven by the wind that whistled through the swaying trees. A tree had fallen on the electricity wires plunging the village and hotel into darkness, and the handful of guests had already retired to their beds.

I felt small and vulnerable, even afraid, as I gazed in awe as the storm's power and intensity destroyed anything with weak foundations that stood in its way. As it raged, creating its mayhem, it reflected my own inner storm. I had only been at the hotel for six months and already things had gone wrong. My dreams and expectations were being torn apart, and I felt as powerless to change the situation at the hotel as did the flowers in the face of nature's wrath.

I stood there until the downpour slowly receded into the distance and the heavy black cloud drifted towards Cusco. With my body pumping adrenaline I locked up the little office and walked down the long stone steps to the railway tracks and beyond, towards the Urubamba River, as if some unseen force was pulling me in the direction I needed to go. Turning left, the opposite way to the village of Aguas Calientes, I began to walk along the tracks and into the darkness. Everything was shrouded in a dark thick cloak. There was no moon, no stars, just the roar of the river and its white gleaming spray breaking the darkness.

I walked into the black void, my mind free, liberated from its constant negative chattering, possessed by an inner energy that controlled my feet. After a few hours the mountains seemed less close together, and the plains of the next valley could be seen in the distance. Reaching a stone shimmering with light, that hung over the bank of the river, I decided to stop and rest.

Lying on the rock, I could see the first stars shining through the clouds high up in the cosmos, and hear the sound of night birds and the forest above the river's roar. As I became aware of my surroundings a torrent of distressing memories flooded my mind, washing away the feelings of liberation and freedom I had experienced only moments before. I began to sob with helplessness, remembering the excitement I felt in London and on arrival at the hotel, and the confusion and unhappiness that had transpired since.

I had arrived on the first train of the day at the village of Aguas Calientes, nestled in the valley just below the mountains of Huana Picchu, Putu Kusi and Machu Picchu, utilising all the accessible land, from the mountains above it, to the Urubamba River that flows below. In 1911, the explorer Hiram Bingham discovered Machu Picchu, the only Inca settlement intact and untouched by the Spanish invaders. There are no records of Machu Picchu and so archaeologists can only speculate as to its function. Aguas Calientes was originally built to house the workers employed to restore the archaeological site and build a railway from Cusco to the ruins. Over time, tourists began to visit the area, attracted by the history, the enigma of the site, and the unusual energy of the place.

The first thing that I noticed was the clean, fresh, pure air. No road has been built from Cusco to Machu Picchu, so the only way to Aguas Calientes is by train. The railway journey northwards from Cusco is breathtaking, as the train winds its way through the Andes ranges. My heart began to beat faster with anticipation as we neared the village. The mountains, towering above, were drawn together, until there was only the railway track and the river cutting through them. Orchids, colourful busy lizzies, and the most incredible red flowers grew from the side of the mountains, giving them a wonderful rainbow of colours that blended with the deep green of the grasses. The occasional condor swooped past, riding a gust of wind, its huge wings spread out as it soared the sky.

A tarmac road from the village runs parallel to the river, and then snakes up the mountain to the ruins a kilometre away. Alternatively, the original Inca path can be walked. Restaurants and hotels line the route, as well as the main square. At the end of the main road are the natural volcanic hot water springs from which the village derives its name. These have been converted into baths for swimming, where the sulphuric water has been known to cure skin ailments and heal wounds. Alongside these volcanic pools runs an ice-cold tributary that descends from the top of the mountains and empties into the Urubamba River. Aguas Calientes reminded me of one of the last frontier towns, dotted with unfinished buildings and hotels erected without thought to order, mirroring the wild, uncontrollable energy of the place and adding to its unique charm.

During the day the village is always full of noise and activity - locals selling their goods, from ethnic bags to clothes and all types of indigenous memorabilia, boys playing football on the pitch near the school, tourists munching pizza while waiting for the train out, children laughing and playing in the square, and dogs barking. I fell in love with the place immediately, feeling that there were many opportunities to make a difference in this small, chaotic place. I had high expectations for myself, and what I wanted to achieve.

However, I started out on the wrong foot almost immediately by making an enemy of the General Manager, and I didn't know how to put things right. After a few days he had begun to make sexual advances towards me. The machismo culture of Peru was frustrating, and I was less forgiving than the Peruvian women, rejecting his proposals with a disgusted look and an air of indifference that only served to incense him. In his anger he began to make my life very difficult. Slowly he spread rumours and gossip about me that I was unaware of and could not defend. He would deliberately exclude me from the small group of hotel workers by organising staff meals, and I would only find out when I heard their laughter coming from the kitchen. Soon groups of girls would whisper in corners, and when I approached they would stop talking and walk away. Salsa nights were organised and I would be left in the hotel office alone. The initial language barrier that I had first struggled with had been replaced with a communications barrier that I did not know how to overcome.

Memories and feelings from when I was a teenager unconsciously emerged, and so I reacted the only way I knew how, by pretending not to care and acting as though indifferent to their actions. This was the defence mechanism that I had used for most of my life to protect me from being hurt, but just as before, this behaviour pattern backfired. It gave the impression that I was unfriendly and aloof, adding to my isolation. I could clearly see that I was trapped by my past experiences and the unconstructive emotions they triggered, but was unable to stop this automatic reaction or change my behaviour to try to remedy the situation. Everything seemed hopeless.

\* \* \*

Lying on the rock, all cried out, stillness descended over me, and in that stillness I could finally hear the voice from deep within that had been drowned out by the noise of confusion and despair.

*"Rebecca, Do not fear – you are never given any test you cannot overcome. You can only control the actions of one person and that is yourself. Learn not to constantly seek the approval of others but to listen to your inner voice, and trust it completely. Let go of your attachment to who you THINK you are according to those around you and your own limiting beliefs."*

*"BUT WHO AM I?"* I shouted into the night sky.

*"You are whoever you choose to be."*

*"I thought I could be a successful Cultural and Activities Manager?"* I whispered to the mountains.

*"Trust and you will be guided."* I heard in answer.

I returned to the hotel in a more positive frame of mind, reassured that things would get better. They didn't. It wasn't long before the owners, who continually blocked my ideas, and the other workers, ignored me completely. Obviously no longer welcome at the hotel, I didn't know what to do for the best, being still attached to my dream of working in Machu Picchu. Intending to stay at the hotel for at least a year, I had barely been there six months, and now felt trapped by my expectations. More restless and unhappy than living the treadmill existence in London, the only thing that relieved the pressure was my afternoon run.

\* \* \*

Most afternoons I would go running on one of the mountains that flanked the hotel. The path that criss-crossed up and around the mountainside led me through the orchid garden, past a thicket of tall thin trees, across streams and past waterfalls. Sometimes a snake would pass by or a beautiful bird with rainbow feathers would fly alongside me, singing sweetly, unafraid of this rare intrusion on the secluded mountain.

Climbing higher and higher the foliage got denser and more enclosed, as though I was in a tunnel glowing with green energy. I always knew the plateau was near when a sweet breeze filled my nostrils with the scent of mountain flowers and ferns growing in the sunlight. Suddenly, emerging out of the green darkness, an expanse of blue sky, fluffy clouds and the jagged mountain peaks of the Andes reaching far into the distance would greet me. Reaching the top my heart would leap, free, safe and far away from all my troubles down below.

There was nothing to prepare me for what was about to happen on this particular day except my state of mind. It was raining, the grey, stormy day reflecting my mood completely. An argument with the General Manager, who had again blocked another of my proposals, had left me feeling caged, limited and frustrated. Running on the usual path out of the hotel complex I began following its winding trail to the mountain, when suddenly, out of the corner of my eye, I noticed an animal track to the left of me leading up a different mountainside.

The path seemed to vibrate, and without consciously making the decision I took a steep left and began to follow it, wondering why I had never noticed it before. After about half an hour the path ended, leaving only bush and shrubs with a few trees dotted around. I was sure that I would rediscover the trail further on. Pulling myself higher and higher, using the shrubs and bushes to help lever myself up, I was so absorbed with the task of climbing, as if in deep meditation, that time seemed to stop. Eventually, I reached a sort of plateau and threw myself onto the grass to rest. My arms and legs ached and I was breathing deeply. The rain had stopped and the sun was burning away the last of the grey clouds. I slowly turned around to see the view and my heart leapt into my mouth.

The mountain on the other side of the valley no longer towered above me. I was now at the same height as its peak. Looking back at the way I had come I realised just how far I had climbed, but there was no sign of my trail at all. The way looked untouched. I tried to work out how I was going to get down, but was too physically and mentally exhausted to think clearly. Glancing to my left and noticing that the tall grass was dotted with funnel webs, I began to panic as it dawned on me that there were poisonous spiders and snakes living on this deserted mountain. I was the intruder. After weighing up the options, I decided to go around the mountain and make my way down the other side of it in the hope of coming across a path or track of some kind.

As I slowly made my way across the mountain it became obvious that this route was more perilous than the way I had come, but it was too late to turn back. Clambering down the mountainside I prayed desperately that a path would appear, or that something would protect me from falling. But no path magically appeared. Instead, as the sun began to set behind the opposite mountains, the grass and bushes petered out, leaving only smooth rock. The further I descended the more precarious the way became until I had reached the point of real danger, and didn't know where to put the next step. I had to face the inevitable truth that I was about to fall.

My mind went numb, unable to cope with the reality of my situation. The faith that everything would turn out all right had proved fruitless, both at the hotel, and now on this mountainside. A sob rose from the depths of me as I realised I was completely alone, and that I could die out here. No one could save me now. Peering down I could only see rock flanking the mountain, smooth and shiny from the rain. My left foot slipped. In wild panic my hands flailed to find a hold on anything to stop myself from falling. But there was nothing and before I knew what was happening I was tumbling down the mountainside out of control.

My heart raced as I went into freefall down the rock face. Falling, falling. The wind whistled past my ears and the smell of fresh rain and wet stone filled my nostrils. I called to the mountain to help me. Save me. I wasn't ready to die. Time seemed to expand as my journey in Machu Picchu flashed before me and I saw with absolute clarity that there was still so much more I had to achieve and experience in Peru, and that it was time to leave the hotel without needing to know what would happen next

As the decision formed I realised I had stopped falling. Looking down in disbelief I saw that I had landed on a tree trunk jutting out of the side of the mountain. Tears of relief ran down my face. The tree had broken my fall and I was not going to die, despite falling at least thirty metres down the rock face, and looking up a bubble of joy exploded within me. I was gloriously energised, full of the life that I had come so close to losing.

Having been given another chance my faith was strong again, and knowing I would not be hurt I fell the last five metres to the base of the mountain and got up, scratched and bruised, but otherwise uninjured. My mind was silent, numbed into submission, my body trembling as I realised how close I had been to really hurting myself. More importantly, the fall had jolted me awake just in time to become aware of all the doors and opportunities that were about to open.

* * *

Walking out onto the balcony I lit a cigarette and took a long, deep drag. I had been hunched over the computer for nearly three hours, immersed in the Internet. The cool dark night was moist with the coming rains, and breathing in the sweet air I could feel the bruised and aching muscles in my shoulders and back relax. The cuts and scrapes from my fall down the mountain earlier that day were beginning to irritate but nothing could disturb the feeling of peace that flowed through my body. Fluffy clouds scuttled across the full moon, which cast a strange white glowing light on the mountains, giving them an aura that pulsated and made them look alive. I took in the scene before me - the towering mountains that reached to the heavens, surrounding me on all sides, the roar of the ancient Urubamba river below, cutting a fine line through the valley, and the lights of the village of Aguas Calientes twinkling in the distance. A sense of peace pervaded the valley accentuating my own feeling of well-being.

When first arriving at the hotel I had been afraid of these towering monsters that represented the huge challenges I had to overcome, but having become accustomed to living in their shadow, I now had to leave them. It was time to accept that I had to move on. But I was scared and suddenly felt the weight of all the failures in my life well up and threaten to consume me as I saw the inadequacies that had never allowed me to truly be myself. "Please lead me to where I need to be for my highest good and to the people that can show me the way. May I find what I am looking for," I prayed, not knowing who to – I had lost my faith in God a long time ago - but surprising myself with this spontaneous heart-felt plea. As if in answer an unusually chilly wind blew across the balcony, sending a shiver down my spine.

I felt my body prickle with apprehension, and the scene in front of me seemed to fade, as if a veil had been thrown across the mountains and the river. Everything became ominously quiet and still. Time stopped, and, as if in a dream, another dimension opened up before my eyes.

The veil between my rational world and the world of magic, the other dimensions, that we as humans rarely have the honour of experiencing, had lifted. A vision appeared and from the nucleus of the vision the form of a presence filled the space where the mountains had been. There was nothing tangible that I could see with my physical eyes, it was more a feeling, a barely perceptible outline of a person that I felt I knew on an inner level.

There was no sound, but from the vision I heard his voice, which boomed around my brain and resonated through every cell of my body. "To find who you truly are, you must let go of all your dreams and expectations and come to me. I am waiting for you. Your destiny is here in the Amazon."

"But why the Amazon? Surely my destiny is here in Machu Picchu," I questioned the apparition before me.

"Your time in Machu Picchu was only to prepare you. Your destiny has always been with me and now you are almost ready."

"Ready for what?" I thought. "What is my purpose for being in Peru?"

"Ready to find out who you truly are," came the reply.

"What is my destiny?"

"Be patient, all your questions will be answered in time,"

"Shall I come now?" I asked.

"You need to learn one thing more before you can leave. It will come as a message. Be open to the message and then you will be ready to meet me."

Slowly, the vision evaporated. The mountain forms reappeared and the roar of the river again echoed around the valley. My body started to tremble and my mind went blank. I was dazed and confused, unsure of what had just happened. I was shivering as cold chills ran up and down my spine. My heart pounded like a herd of buffalo on the African plains as it frantically pumped hot blood around my body. I was energised, but also terrified, as I gripped the side of the balcony for support.

The vision and the words "To find who you truly are, you must let go of all your dreams and expectations and come to me," continued to echo around my mind. The message was clear. In order to truly find myself I had to let go of the need for the approval of others, and my own limited and conditioned beliefs about who I was. Machu Picchu had prepared me by destroying my dreams about being successful. I now had direction. I was just fearful of the Amazon. It represented all I was scared of, the unknown, change, and having to face that which I knew I had to let go of.

\* \* \*

The very next day I received confirmation that the vision was more than just a figment of my imagination in the shape of a gift. The General Manager, of all people, gave me a book to read called *One River*, that charts the adventures of a Harvard biologist called Wade Davis who followed the route his teacher, Richard Evan Shultz, made through the Colombian and Peruvian Amazon, mapping the various natural rubber plantations for the American government. During his interactions with the indigenous tribes Shultz had come in contact with the visionary vine Ayahuasca, and the author chronicles his, and his teacher's, journeys and experiences with this sacred medicine.

After reading the book, I instinctively knew that the vision was a calling from a shaman who would take me on an Ayahuasca initiation, just like this adventurer, Richard Evan Shultz, and that Iquitos, the capital city of the Peruvian rainforest in the North-East of Peru and the gateway to the Amazon, was the obvious place to go. Once the decision was made the sign I was waiting for arrived in the shape of a large and buxom healer. She was an American lady with vibrant energy and an aura of peace around her who visited the hotel annually with groups to take ceremonies on top of Machu Picchu. The moment we saw each other we both knew she had come to give me something. After I had settled her in we agreed to meet later that night.

She called me to her room at midnight, and I arrived eager to hear any message she may have for me. I entered the room and she sat me down opposite her on the floor. After some time she broke the comfortable silence. "Well Rebecca, we meet at the right time, for you have reached a crossroad and the door is now open for you to walk a different path with new possibilities. I am here to give you a gift, for I can see there is still some fear despite all that you have been shown. Remember that life is only the result of the choices that we make at every moment. You now have the opportunity to meet your destiny. It is a promise you made before entering your body, but first I must show you something".

She settled me on some cushions and then put her hand on my back. Immediately, I felt a warm surge of energy through my body and my mind cleared of all thoughts. As the heat began to intensify and flow through me I began to lose consciousness of my surroundings.

I had the sensation that I was riding a horse; the feeling of fear was very strong, and I began to rock involuntarily as though riding very fast. An unknown person was chasing me and I was in danger. I began to sob, as I saw that my death was imminent and that the person chasing me would kill me. At this point my body was physically leaping up and down quite on its own accord. I was out of breath and felt a deep exhaustion overwhelm me. I was going to die, die, die and then everything went black.

Out of the gloom came a skeleton and I knew it was me, time and time again, dying and death, dying and death, lifetime after lifetime. I was flooded with realisations, I had died and for what – a pointless death, a pointless life full of suffering? To live and die again without achieving anything consciously, forgetting to live until I was about to die.

And then I saw what my subconscious had struggled to remember when I had received the message from the Shaman. There was an end to this mad cycle of death and rebirth. It was when we remembered who we truly were.

Slowly I could feel myself back in the hotel room with the

healer. My eyes and heart had been re-opened, and I fully and consciously remembered why I had come to Peru. I had come to Machu Picchu under the pretext that I would achieve a successful career in tourism after all my failures and had forgotten that I had come to learn about healing. Instead, I had responded to the challenges with past emotional reactions and had remained in my pain – a victim. My ego had been battered and broken, all my dreams and expectations of who I should be had been shattered. I had lost everything and now I had nothing to lose but to walk on into the unknown.

I was ready to follow my vision. I didn't know who this person was I was meant to meet, but suddenly the details no longer mattered. My search for my true identity was about to begin again, and all I needed to do was believe that the magic would lead me to where I had to go. The magic had led me to the hotel and to Machu Picchu, to the mountains and the Urubamba River, and to this healer, and now it was leading me to the next place.

Two days after the experience with the healer, as I was trying to figure out how to leave, an unexpected call came. The General Manager told me that I had twenty-four hours to leave the hotel, giving no reason. I didn't need one. My bags were already packed in preparation, and I was relieved that it was so soon. I was ready.

\* \* \*

The following day a motley crew of about five people turned up at the train station to send me off on the last train out of Aguas Calientes. The guard rang his bell and I leaned out of the window to wave goodbye. As the train began to chug out of the station my heart did a leap, for the ending, and the new beginning.

I was filled with excited apprehension as the train made its way to Cusco. I cast my mind back to when I had first arrived all those months before. How young I was then. So much had happened to help me see myself more clearly. I felt older and wiser, and as the train wound round each bend taking me further from the Andes ranges, I said a silent thank you for the special experiences that I'd had there. For the times alone, for the runs in the mountains, for the midnight walks, for the early meditation sessions, and for the wonderful people I had met at the hotel who had helped me on my journey.

As the sun died over the mountains it cast a deep red glow on the snow-covered tips and the air chilled my face. Time had not stopped, now it was winter, and the tourists would start flooding in. With the change of seasons I was heading towards a new horizon, to keep my date with destiny.

# CHAPTER THREE

## *Believing in the Dream*

Accelerating down the runway I gripped the armrests and looked out of the window as the airport raced before my eyes. The plane shuddered as it slowly lifted off the tarmac into the sky, and Lima was left far below. Two weeks after leaving the hotel I was on my way to Iquitos, heading to where I believed I would find the Shaman – in one of the most ancient places on this planet – the Peruvian Amazon. I peered out of the window as the plane began to descend, and saw a blanket of green below, with rivers slicing across it as far as the eye could see. I suddenly felt a surge of impatience to find out if the vision was real, or had only been a figment of my over-active imagination.

The airport was hot and humid despite the air conditioning, and outside a rain shower was slowly dying away into the horizon. The sun had come out and the whole of the rainforest steamed like a hot oven. As I stepped out of the airport, sweating profusely and overwhelmed by the smell of lush green vegetation, I saw an army of touts shouting and jostling for attention. I saw them pounce on a number of inexperienced fellow travellers and looked around frantically to find a taxi before they spotted me.

A man appeared in front of me almost immediately. "You go to Iquitos? I take you to good hotel," he said in English. We agreed a price and grabbing my bag he plunged into the crowd.

I followed, dazed and overwhelmed as we passed by the huge selection of tours, lodges and rainforest experiences on offer. We reached the car park and I looked in disbelief as he bundled me into a very ancient car. There was no flooring, the paintwork had disintegrated, and it looked ready to fall apart at any moment. Seeing my face the taxi driver laughed, "Don't worry, still a few more years left in this baby yet." His Americanism just added to my shock. As we trundled out of the airport and into the city I looked around me in confusion.

Where were the indigenous women carrying children slung onto their backs, and the men dressed in traditional headdresses and tribal clothes, carrying machetes and living in communities surrounded by jungle that I had always imagined in my mind? I was surprised by my own expectations of how the rainforest should be.

Instead, Iquitos is a bustling market city that can only be reached by air or river with a population of about 400,000 people. Growing from a small settlement of Jesuit missionaries in the 1700s, Iquitos became important during the rubber boom of the late nineteenth century. By the end of the First World War the rubber boom had died, with plantations in the Malay Peninsula capturing the world market. A period of decline followed until the 1960s when oil was discovered, catapulting Iquitos into the prosperous modern city it is today.

The taxi driver insisted that he take me to a very safe and cheap hotel, which turned out to be a dreary, dark building in the middle of nowhere. I was led to a concrete room with a fan and small bed. The hotel seemed deserted and it appeared that I was the only guest, but I was too tired to find another. Although the sun had gone down the heat was oppressive and the humidity almost unbearable. I flopped onto the bed and closed my eyes, as the wind of the fan cooled my sweating body. After resting for a while I had a cold shower and changed into some cotton clothes. I felt much better and realised that I was hungry. The hotel manager directed me in the general direction of the tourist restaurants. Taking a deep breath, I plunged into the thick heat and headed for the Amazon River.

The streets were wide, and busy with rickshaws, little three-wheel cabs that can only be found in Iquitos, taxis, and thousands of motorbikes - the preferred mode of travel. The city was alive with rainforest energy car horns beeping, children screaming, dogs barking, and sellers shouting their wares created a symphony of sounds, and despite my exhaustion I began to feel revitalised by the bustling life around me.

After about fifteen minutes walk I reached the area with the tourist restaurants and saw Westerners walking around. Knowing I had to be close to the river my heart began to beat faster. I walked down a street lined with salsa clubs and pizza restaurants that merged into a pedestrian walkway crowded with people. Merging with the throng I was suddenly hit by a sight I shall never forget. The huge Amazon River was stretched out before me as far as the eye could see, the sky blanketed with stars and the sliver of a new moon, which took my breath away.

This magnificent river produces twenty per cent of all the water, and has the highest volume of freshwater, that pours into the world's oceans. A cacophony of insect sounds and frog callings accompanied the shouts and noise of the humans milling along its edge. I walked along the promenade marvelling at the clowns, jugglers, and street performers making the crowds laugh, the couples walking arm in arm, children eating ice cream and playing, and the bars and restaurants filled with tourists and locals having a good time.

Everyone was smiling and laughing, and for the first time since I had been in Peru I felt safe and secure. A warm glow filled my body, and I felt an urge to just sit by the river, awed by the sheer expanse of sky and horizon. I wanted to hug myself in glee and delight, having accomplished my part of the bargain. I had made it to Iquitos, gateway to the Amazon.

Destiny now had to fulfil its part, as I had no idea how I would find the presence that had called me here to this huge rainforest. I wasn't sure what I needed to do next. On the way to the Amazon River I had passed many shops selling Ayahuasca journeys with shaman, offering the authentic 'Shamanic Experience' but they all seemed very money-orientated and non-spiritual. Looking out across the vast expanse of river I suddenly heard in my head *"you don't need to do anything. Just let go and believe and you will be led to the right place at the right time. Have faith, enjoy your time here in Iquitos, and you will find what you are looking for. Do nothing: it will find you."*

All I could do was surrender to the magic. Sitting on the wall looking out at the wondrous view and sipping a cold beer, my heart filled with love and gratitude to something greater than myself. Tomorrow no longer mattered. I had made it today, and was closer to my dream then ever before.

\* \* \*

There was only one restaurant where the tourists gathered to eat good western food. It was here that people met to exchange stories and adventures, share information or find a tourist guide for some specific rainforest experience. It was always packed, with lively and interesting debates going on at most of the tables. One night at supper, a few days after I had arrived, an American approached and asked if he could join me. I was grateful for the company having kept very much to myself, not meeting many people. He introduced himself as Michael, and he told me he had been coming to Iquitos and the Amazon for years because of his fascination with shamanism and the medicinal plant Ayahuasca.

Michael told me that shaman are practitioners that have access to the supernatural realms and direct contact with the spirit world. By ingesting certain plant medicine they are able to go on a 'shamanic journey' and enter different realities and dimensions, seeking knowledge and utilising healing power from the spirit beings. In South America, the shaman are believed to have the power to deflect and neutralise evil, and diagnose sickness by using the healing properties of tobacco, and more specifically, Ayahuasca.

The name Ayahuasca is from the South American Indian language of *Quechua*. *Aya* means 'souls', 'dead people' or 'spirits' and *huasca* means 'vine' or 'liana'. In English, it is translated as 'vine of the dead' or 'vine of the soul.' The shaman believe that humans have come from the cosmos and the 'vine of the soul' was given to them to enable them to remain in contact with the cosmic and solar creative energies.

Ayahuasca is a brew made up of two essential ingredients. The hallucinogenic properties of Ayahuasca, that provide the access to the spirit world and the visions, come from the leaves of the *Psychotria viridis*, containing the hormone *dimethyltryptamine* (DMT), which is naturally secreted in the human brain. DMT, when taken orally however, is broken down by the *monoamine oxidase* (MAO) enzyme in the stomach. To prevent this the *Banisteropsis caapi*, a vine, is mixed with the leaves, which protects the DMT from this MAO. The shaman can alter the brew by adding or taking away various different leaves from the *Banisteropsis caapi* vine.

There are over 80,000 known species of plants in the Amazon and 3,700,000,000 possible combinations to find effective remedies. Amazonian shaman recognise that Ayahuasca is more than just medicine - it is also a teacher. It imparts vital medicinal knowledge by becoming the communicator between the plant and the shaman, with instructions on which plants work best together for healing and cures. Michael had just read a book that had explained that the image of 'huge twisting serpents' at the centre of the Ayahuasca vision are actually a metaphor for the strands of DNA, the molecular coding for every living thing on this planet. The author proposed that the DNA double twisting serpents were at the source of shamanic knowledge, allowing the shaman to communicate with animate objects at the molecular level.

The Ayahuasca tradition and the knowledge it contains have been handed down for thousands of years. Each shaman has been initiated through a diligent period of apprenticeship and maintains and increases the power of Ayahuasca through physical healing. This ancient knowledge and wisdom has also been preserved to maintain human contact with the other dimensions that exist beyond what we can see with the physical eye. Ayahuasca enables the shaman to heal using the essential 'medicines' of Faith, Prayer and Belief, powerful medicines that have been forgotten by Western scientific medicine in the need to make more profit. Over time, Michael had noticed an increased interest in taking the vine by Westerners and the rise in Ayahuasca tourism. He found it interesting that as we are becoming more separated from the sacred and spiritual dimensions, we are unconsciously searching for it, knowing it exists and needing to reconnect with it.

I wanted to know if it was still possible to take Ayahuasca in traditional ceremony with a genuine shaman. According to Michael it was, and he had met a few people who had stayed with tribes, but it was very rare. There seemed to be more charlatans than authentic shaman and it was becoming very difficult to find a shaman that hadn't been tempted by money and prestige. Many had let the adulation by Westerners looking for gurus and teachers take precedence over the teachings, and were no longer powerful. However, Ayahuasca was still widely recognised as probably the most powerful plant medicine available at the present time on the planet, for it not only heals on the physical level but also spiritually, emotionally and psychologically. Michael assured me that if the vision I had experienced in Machu Picchu had been real, all I needed to do was put it out in intention and the right teacher would appear.

Handing me the book called the *Cosmic Serpent - DNA and the Origins of Knowledge* by James Narby, Michael told me that it held all the answers to my questions regarding this visionary vine. He was leaving early in the morning to fly back to the States. The book had only just come out in print and he told me I was fortunate to have a copy before going into the rainforest.

As he said this goose bumps appeared all over my body. This book was going to prepare me for whatever lay ahead. It was the first clear sign that I was heading in the right direction. Thanking Michael I left the restaurant and hurried to the Amazon River. Sitting on the wall in my favourite spot, a relatively secluded area further down from the restaurants overlooking the river, I was soon engrossed in the book. The more I read the more I realised that it was this plant medicine, Ayahuasca, that held the answers to all my questions. I just needed to find the right teacher.

* * *

While I waited for something to happen I tried to keep myself as busy as possible. I visited the Museo Regional, the Puerto Almendras, the Library, the Laguna Moronacocha, and Laguna Quistacocha just outside Iquitos, swimming and relaxing with the Peruvian day- trippers. I also spent many hours of the week by the riverfront, soaking up its magnificence, trying to decipher its unique sounds and mesmerised by the myriad of colours that change constantly, depending on the position of the sun and the clouds. During these times I envisioned myself with a shaman, a teacher, somewhere in the Amazon, taking Ayahuasca. Occasionally, when I became doubtful, I would remind myself of the experiences in Machu Picchu and of meeting Michael. Often the words that I had heard on my first night in Iquitos; *do nothing: it will find you*, vibrated around my head, making me feel strong and calm again.

After ten days of exploring I was running out of things to do, and was no closer to discovering the vision. The few tourists I had met all had somewhere to go and something to do, a rainforest lodge or expedition of some kind. A couple of people asked me if I would like to join them, but I declined, waiting patiently for the sign that would show me the way, but I was slowly beginning to doubt the vision.

After two weeks had gone by panic was setting in. The peace and hope felt when I first arrived in Iquitos had been replaced by a fear that I was deluding myself completely. I began to believe that the vision had just been a mad figment of my imagination. Maybe it was all wishful thinking and now I was stuck in the middle of the Amazon, my dreams shattered.

In my desperation I decided to be more active, rather than just trusting the process as the message had said. I began to talk to various travellers and Westerners living in Iquitos about the rational possibilities of taking Ayahuasca with an authentic shaman. It quickly became apparent that there didn't seem to be much hope, as indigenous people were not accessible to travellers.

Most suggested going to stay in a rainforest lodge that had an in-house shaman – but warned that most of these were charlatans of the worst kind. I swallowed my pride and explored the possibilities, but none of the lodges that offered a shaman seemed right. I was advised that the *'Centro Latino American de Relaciones Humanas e Interculturas'* might be able to help me, and made the journey by rickshaw to the centre. After waiting around for what seemed like hours, I eventually got an appointment with one of the Europeans who was working there.

Sitting opposite me, his huge desk separating us physically and mentally, he nodded sagely as I explained that I wanted to stay with indigenous people. At the last minute I omitted telling him about the vision, and was relieved that I had. He let me finish, and then fixing me with his cold blue eyes let forth a torrent of what I can only believe to be pent up frustration. He ranted to me about the problems of over enthusiastic travellers with inflated perceptions of indigenous people and shaman. There was no such thing as the 'authentic experience' as all the accessible rainforest people were *matizos* – local people who had emigrated there.

He hammered the final nail in my coffin of doubt by telling me that there was no possible way of working or living with indigenous people unless I was part of an academic project and found my own funding. Even then I still didn't have the right academic qualifications to be seriously considered. "My suggestion to you is to forget about staying with an indigenous family. Go and stay in one of the many lodges in the rainforest and have some fun. They are all more or less the same," were his passing words to me.

I left his office feeling totally defeated. Waiting for the bus back to the hotel I made a decision to leave Iquitos the next morning. Perhaps I was in the wrong country and would have better luck in Letitcia – the rainforest capital of Colombia. Anything seemed better then waiting another day in Peru for nothing to happen. The faith in my dream and the vision were lost in the words of the professor, a rational man who obviously knew more than me about the workings of the rainforest.

I returned to the hotel, and after a cold shower felt better. Deciding to make my peace with the river and say goodbye, I walked the now familiar way to the waterfront. Sitting at my favourite spot, I breathed in the scent of the Amazon and all the muscles in my body relaxed.

Closing my eyes, I wished that Harry were with me to comfort and tell me it was going to be all right. Leaving him had been the hardest thing to do. We had been together for over a year and were still madly in love. Harry, in his wisdom, knew that he could not stop me from going to Peru and following my dream. He was following his own dreams in Germany, and our separation had bought us even closer together.

Supporting me when I told him about my vision in Machu Picchu, he insisted that I fly to Iquitos. His belief in me had been so strong, and now I was letting him down by no longer believing in myself. Tears sprung to my eyes as a deep sensation welled up in my stomach. I was losing my faith in the dream, and longed to feel Harry's warm protective hands holding me and hear his sweet words of love.

"He loves you completely and will be with you every step of the way."

Startled out of my reverie I opened my eyes to find a local man sitting next to me on the wall, dressed in white linen trousers and an orange t-shirt. His skin was very dark and his long black hair was tied in a ponytail. Indian heritage was clearly defined in a face that was wide and flat with sharp cheekbones, ageless and timeless.

"Excuse me. Did you say something?" I asked him.

He fixed his incredibly clear blue/green eyes on mine and a smile played on his lips.

"Yes, I said he loves you completely and will be with you every step of the way." I looked at this stranger in shock. Could this man read my mind? How did he know that I was thinking about Harry?

"What do you mean?" I spluttered.

"I am talking about God. Whenever I look at this river I remember God is always looking down at us and loving us, regardless of what we do or the mistakes we have made".

I breathed a sigh of relief. At least my thoughts were still sacred and private.

*"Dios es Grande,"* he said.

"I know what you mean. When we see nature in its full glory like this God becomes more real. But does he really exist or is he just a safety net for the insecurity of an ever changing world?" I blurted out, surprised at opening up immediately to this stranger. He didn't seem to mind at all and after a moment he answered in a voice that reflected wisdom.

"God is as real as you believe Him to be. He exists if you want Him to exist. But He is only one answer to one question. There are as many questions and as many answers as there are stars above us."

Simultaneously, we both stared up, and at that moment a shooting star blazed a trail across the night sky. We sat in silence marvelling at the wonder of space. My companion's voice broke the stillness.

"We have been blessed tonight. A shooting star is a good sign that our dreams will be coming true. Tell me, what is your dream?"

"How do you know I have a dream?" I asked.

"Well, it has been written in the stars," he replied with a laugh.

I laughed with him. There was something familiar about this softly spoken man with the blue/green eyes. I felt that I could tell him anything, and suddenly opened up to this stranger about my experiences in Machu Picchu, the vision, and my search for a teacher. I expected him to laugh out loud or look at me in disbelief, but instead his face became serious and he seemed to be deep in thought. Closing his eyes he started to nod his head slowly, as though agreeing to something. Opening them again he stared right at me, looking deep into my soul. It took all my will power not to look away.

"Yes, you will find your teacher. Believe and you shall find. Have strength, courage and love in your heart and you will be led to where you need to go. It is your destiny and you are being guided. Remember, when your intentions and motives are real and pure the universal energy works to help you. People will enter your life to show you the way. All you need to do is trust the process."

"But how will I know if these people are here to help me or not?" I asked, thinking of the healer in Machu Picchu, and

Michael and the book he had given me and then about all the others who had told me my dreams were impossible. How did I know who to believe and who to doubt?

"Only you have the answers inside you. Only you know your Truth. Sometimes the difficulty is in hearing *and* believing it. Many do not follow their dreams because they are too fearful of change and letting go. Attachment and fear leads people to listen to those that have a different agenda or different life experiences, and so cannot help them. You will know whom to believe when the words that are spoken resonate deep inside the core of you, or gifts are given to help you on your path," the man answered, as if reading my thoughts.

I thought about the contrast between my meeting with Michael and my meeting with the professor at the *Centro Latino American de Relaciones Humanas e Interculturas*. When I had met Michael I still believed that the dream would happen, so his experiences had resonated with my truth. The book he had given me was a gift, and a sign that I was on the right path. I had met the professor when I was beginning to feel that it was an impossible dream, and he had only reflected my own fears. Fears that still overwhelmed me.

"But what if it doesn't happen. How do I know if my dreams are real or just wishful thinking?"

"The key is to have complete trust," he replied. "Even a speck of doubt stops the dream becoming a reality. You have made it to the Amazon. You are so close. Now all you can do is trust."

"But it is so difficult to trust an intangible dream that only exists in the heart. How is it possible to follow a dream with complete faith?" I said, voicing my frustrations.

"Ah! You are asking the wrong question. You need to ask yourself who do you want to be? And when you ask this question you have a profound choice. You can decide to be the person you think you are supposed to be, or the person other people want you to be, or the person you have always hoped to discover you actually are. You must summon the courage to manifest your true potential and respond to what's in your heart. Only then can you find your way. Patience, courage and faith are necessary to find what you are looking for. The more you walk with conviction, the more you follow your path, the more the people that hold you back will fall away. Do not be scared to walk alone in your truth. You understand this?" he asked, looking at me.

"What does it mean to walk in your truth?" I answered. "It sounds so easy, but I'm not even sure what my truth is," I answered.

"Never compromise your dreams. We are all born to be free. It is the destiny of every single person on this planet. It is our divine right, otherwise life has no meaning," he replied.

We sat in peaceful silence, the turmoil in my heart dissolving into the warm glow of trust and faith. I didn't know if what this man had said was really the truth, but he sounded like he knew what he was talking about, and I couldn't deny that I was feeling much better about being in Iquitos. I closed my eyes, and a well of deep love and gratitude for the stranger with blue/green eyes welled up from my heart and consumed me. I opened my eyes to thank him for his wisdom and insight, but he had gone, vanished into the night leaving me sitting on the wall on my own.

The next morning the doubt had returned, and I decided to enquire about crossings from Iquitos to the Colombian port of Letitica, eight hours by speedboat across the Amazon. The woman informed me that the next day's boat to Leticia was full, so I put my name down on the waiting list and was told to return later that afternoon, when she would know whether there was a place for me. Slowly I walked to the main square. If I were meant to be in Columbia I would almost certainly get a seat on the speedboat.

Sitting under a tree I became immersed in the scene around me. The square was full of people. There were young lovers enjoying the leafy shade, children selling sweets and cigarettes from large trays that they carried on their chest; fruit sellers balancing huge baskets of watermelon, apples, bananas, coconut and many other exotic and indigenous rainforest fruits on their heads, and young men hoping to get laid.

From across the square I noticed a man in his late twenties staring at me. When he caught my eye he beckoned me over. I shook my head. The last thing I needed was to have the usual conversation with a Peruvian man wanting to practice his English, on possibly my last afternoon in Peru. As I saw him get up and start to come over I spotted a young boy of about eight years old carrying a box and a stool. I called him over and pointed to my filthy walking boots. All over Peru young children earn a living by shining shoes. Most of the kids are great fun, and if you speak Spanish they are not at all shy. This boy was the leader of a group of about five shoe shiners, and before long they had all crowded around me, laughing and joking.

After fifteen minutes my boots were gleaming, and the boys drifted away. There was the man, still waiting patiently. I couldn't avoid him any longer. Sitting beside me I saw his tourist identification card swing on the chain around his neck, denoting that he was a legitimate tourist guide and spoke English. He introduced himself as Javier and told me that he had often seen me sitting by the river's edge, and wanted to know why I had come to the Amazon, and why I was still here in Iquitos.

He had spotted me when I first arrived, and was curious to know why a foreign woman, travelling alone, had not arranged a rainforest tour or a jungle lodge. I was surprised at his seemingly genuine enquiry, and told him I was not interested in staying at a lodge, or some tourist resort. Before I could stop myself, I explained that I wanted to take Ayahuasca with a traditional shaman, in a rainforest village, away from the main tourist route, but did not know where to go to find one.

He stared at me for some time and then said, "I know the perfect guide for you. His name is Julio, a good friend of mine.

He takes tourists to a family on a small tributary in the rainforest, to take Ayahuasca with a shaman who lives there. But the conditions are very difficult. If you do not mind roughing it, maybe he could take you." As he talked my heart started to pound and blood rushed to my ears. It was all so perfect, and it made sense to go with a professional guide who would protect me. Maybe the Shaman was in Peru after all, and this guide Julio would take me to him. Hardly containing my excitement, I asked Javier where I could find this guide.

"Julio works for himself and is sometimes here, sometimes there, sometimes he works and at other times he doesn't. I haven't seen him for a while, so he has probably been in the rainforest with some tourists," he replied, somewhat surprised by the change in my demeanour.

Now that my dream had the possibility of coming true I suddenly felt full of anxiety. This was the sign I had been waiting for. His words had resonated deep within me. "I really need to find him. I must. At least we can have a look for him. Please can you help me?" I asked breathlessly, and seeing the look of desperation on my face, he agreed.

We hopped into a passing rickshaw and checked out all of Julio's usual haunts. No one had seen or heard from him for a few weeks. After scouring most of the cafes and bars in Iquitos, Javier suggested we called it a day. He could see I was frantic, but there was nothing more we could do. I was so close and still it all seemed so far away. He promised to get Julio to contact me when he saw him again. I was hot and exhausted, and seeing that Javier was too, offered to buy him a drink and some lunch by the river to thank him for his help. He suggested a local restaurant, and as we pulled up to it Javier pointed at a table that seated two western women and a Peruvian. "That's Julio," Javier whispered to me, and then he added "*Dios es Grande.*"

After the introductions had been made, we found out that Julio had only arrived back in Iquitos that afternoon. He had been gone for three weeks with a large group, and was now free to take another trip. He had never taken only one tourist (especially a woman) into the rainforest because conditions were so harsh. Despite his reservations he agreed that he would take me to the Shaman's village, acting as my guide, teaching me about rainforest life, and I would have the possibility of taking Ayahuasca with the Shaman.

We arranged to take the next local boat that was departing early in the morning, two days later. Fortunately, this gave me enough time to buy provisions and prepare for the trip, and Julio tried to ready me for what was in store. There were no Western conveniences or luxuries of any kind, no toilets, showers, hot water, drinking water or beds; no sanitation or health care. There were potentially fatal diseases with outbreaks of cholera and influenza; there were dangerous animals and reptiles including huge mosquitoes, giant stinging wasps, poisonous snakes, spiders, rats, biting ants and piranha fish. But I did not care. My dream was one step closer to reality, and soon, if all went according to plan, I would be meeting the Shaman at last.

For the rest of the day I wandered around Iquitos in a daze, not quite believing what had transpired. Just as I was about to give up and try a new direction, the dream had become a reality. But even though I was so close the doubt had not gone. It had only changed, now fuelled by expectations and desires. Every so often it would whisper warnings that everything could still go wrong, that maybe the guide was a liar and the Shaman did not really exist. I tried not to listen to this voice, but during the evening it got stronger and stronger. Trying my best to ignore it, I sorted out the gear for my adventure in the rainforest.

That night I lay awake for a long time, thoughts flowing incessantly around inside my head. Memories of childhood, my unhappiness at school, my suicide attempt, my other travels in India and Asia, and Machu Picchu, all the crossroads that had led me to this point. Everything had worked out perfectly, even when it seemed otherwise, and now my destiny was closer than ever. I had waited so long. I didn't know if I would be able to cope if my dreams fell apart now. As I lay there, torn between faith and doubt, I saw the Shaman as clearly as if he was standing right in front of me. He smiled his big beaming smile and held out his hands to me. "I am waiting for you Rebekita. It is time."

## CHAPTER FOUR

## *The Shaman and his Apprentice*

As I heard the words his face and body became clearer and more defined. He was an old man with chocolate-coloured skin whose round face was beaming with light. His eyes twinkled like two pearls in the moonlight and his cheeks glowed a rosy red. He was small, and dressed in black trousers and a tattered shirt. Puffing on his pipe he looked long and hard at me as he spoke.

"Yes, we meet tomorrow, but do not believe it was luck that brought you to me for there is no such thing as luck. You must take full responsibility for your actions. You've created this reality because it was you alone that made the choices that led you to this point in your life. We are all creating reality, but most do not know they are doing it. Most of us make our choices unconsciously. Your faith in your dream has led you to where you are now."

The vision disappeared but left me feeling as if an electrical charge was flowing up and down my spine. Gradually, the implications of what the Shaman had said started to sink in. Could it be possible that I had created *this* dream and made it a reality just because I believed in it? And if I created this dream, then I had the potential to create any dream. Just before I drifted into sleep a thought struck me. Maybe I *had* created everything in my life but was not aware of it, blinded by the belief that I had no control over the direction of my life.

The next morning, after a restless night, my excitement had been replaced with anxiety. The guide arrived on rainforest time, forty-five minutes late. His eyes were bloodshot and he stank of alcohol. He had been out drinking the night before, was still hung over, and looked like he hadn't gone to bed at all. I had expected him to be early, so was frantic by the time he turned up and angry that he was not more organised, especially as I was paying him additional money because I was travelling alone. I wondered how I was going to spend nine days with a man who had managed to annoy me even before we had left Iquitos. Julio tried to calm me down, telling me that we still had plenty of time before the boat left for the village. He assured me that a friend of his had already put all the supplies we had bought the day before on the boat. There was nothing I could do but trust him.

I had spent the day before in the markets with Julio, buying necessary items that would make my stay in the rainforest more comfortable. These included a machete (an essential tool), Wellington boots, blankets, plastic coverings, hammock, mosquito net, rain cap, mosquito repellent, towels, bleach, toilet paper, toothpaste, toothbrush and shampoo, batteries, soap, towels and tampons, camera film and cassettes. I had also bought one sack of frijoles, one of lentils, two five-kilogram sacks of rice and two big twenty-litre drums of fresh water. This food was considered a gift for the Shaman's family, and a necessity to help me while I accustomed myself to rainforest food and water.

Despite our late departure we stopped off at a little stall before arriving at the chaotic main port of Belen, where boats took travellers to the rainforest villages. Needing fresh supplies we bought onions, garlic, tomatoes, bananas, sugar, tea and coffee. Even though it was still relatively early, the rainforest market was in full flow, heaving with people selling and buying all types of weird and exotic fruits, vegetables, fish and animals, alive and dead.

Once we had reached the main road to the market, it soon became too difficult for our rickshaw to negotiate the flood of human traffic that blocked our path. After a lot of useless swearing and yelling at the hordes of people, my guide began to use his short supply of common sense. He leapt off the rickshaw and impatiently helped me with my rucksack. We each took a bag of groceries, and Julio led the way to the port on foot, expertly dodging the crowds. I just followed as best I could.

I hadn't been to this part of the market, and as I negotiated my way through the masses of people, stray animals and wild children, I couldn't help but look in amazement at the exotic array of produce that was on sale. But we were late and there was no time to stop. I was also in physical discomfort as my left rucksack strap was eating into my shoulder, and sweat poured down my back. Overwhelmed by the heat, pain and stress of the thought that we may miss the boat, I tuned my mind off and concentrated on walking, one foot in front of the other, one foot in front of the other.

As soon as I felt that I could not make another step the guide pointed into the distance. There lay the docks of Belen, where about forty boats were moored ready to take off to different parts of the Amazon, and one of those boats was ours. A sea of people were swarming around the edge of the river trying to find the right boat, looking for lost children or other family members, buying food for their trip, or just selling their wares.

We were very late, and the boat that would take us from Iquitos to the campesino village where the Shaman lived was already heaving with people and full of cargo by the time we arrived. Wearily climbing into the boat, I let out an exhausted sigh of relief. I was out of breath, sweat was running down my back and into my eyes, and my rucksack strap had rubbed the skin away. "Just made it," I thought, as the boat roared its small engine in warning that it was ready to leave.

While we waited to depart, men in canoes paddled up to the

glass-less windows carrying ice boxes filled with bags that contained bright pink sugary drinks, rice, fish and curry, bread and sweets. My stomach began to rumble so I bought a drink and some rainforest bread. The pink liquid was sweet and refreshing, and the bread filled my hunger. Having sufficiently recovered from the walk to the boat, I was able to look around at the chaotic scene in front of me. It was amazing.

The hull was a hive of intense activity and noise. Every inch of space was packed with animals, adults, children and all types of rainforest produce. Angry pigs tied to the posts thrashed underneath the seats, while cocks were tied to the window frames, squawking and flapping their huge wings. The whole floor of the boat was chock-a-block with huge barrels of fish, vegetables and dead animals. Unidentified packages and boxes filled with goods were jammed and stacked so tightly together that there was no floor space to be seen.

Many of the passengers had already strung up their hammocks above the supplies, and children swung fearlessly from the window frames, or sat on the piles of boxes on the floor. Not just every bit of space inside the boat was utilised, but the roof of the boat was also packed with supplies. At one end, twenty desks and chairs had been strapped on for one of the village schools further up the river, and at the other end were endless amounts of coal sacks for one of the richer villages on the tributary. At the very front of the roof were two empty crates turned upside down.

Somewhere in the midst of the packages were my modest supplies. I couldn't see them, but just had to trust that Julio had sorted them out. To my Western eyes it looked totally disorganised, but the Peruvians had a different way of doing things, and I was learning to let go of needing things to be done my way.

I also had other things to worry about, such as coping with the awful stench that I had suddenly become aware of. It did not seem to be affecting anyone else, as I jostled around on the crowded benches trying to find some clean air, but there was no escape. I felt the bile rise in my throat, and my eyes began to water. Praying that the boat would leave soon so that the wind would clear the sickening smell, I silently thanked Julio for being late. The stench was overpowering, and would have been unbearable if we had been on the boat much longer.

Twenty minutes later, and beyond all rational practicality, the captain had defied gravity and space by packing another five families into the cramped hull of the boat. I was green with nausea from the smell and one of the boat employees noticed, inviting me to sit on the crates up on the roof. I was to be given the opportunity to experience the Amazon in her full glory, and observe the wonderful journey to the village in the open air. At last, the boat slowly moved out of Belen port and Captain Shashico expertly manoeuvred it through the channel and into the mouth of the Amazon River.

I had only really seen the Amazon from the walkway in Iquitos, and to be actually on it was another experience entirely. The river is so wide that the horizon took my breath away. I had never seen such a huge expanse of sky, stretching as far as the eye could see, a patchwork of the bluest colours that only nature could possibly conceive. The cloud formations differed depending on what part of the sky I was looking at. Far off to the East there was a huge rain cloud releasing itself onto the rainforest, while above us white fluffy clouds drifted leisurely across the sky, intermittently covering the sun and briefly alleviating its burning rays. Blending into these blue and white hues were the greens of the rainforest, every shade imaginable seemed to pulsate, as the boat sped along the edge of the river.

Huts on the other side of the river were like the model houses that I had collected as a child, and the occasional hint of a pink dolphin appeared and disappeared into the river's dark and gloomy depths. I breathed in deeply, smelling the scent of the

Atlantic Ocean thousands of kilometres away, and savouring the freshness of the air on my lips as the wind whistled past my ears and blew my hair into my eyes.

At around lunchtime we reached a busy intersection where three tributaries joined the Amazon, one of them being the tributary that led to the Shaman's village. Here we stopped to unload cargo and allow more passengers to board the boat for villages up the river, giving existing passengers the opportunity to go to the toilet and buy food. Fresh fish, curry, rice, and all types of meat were on sale, with vegetables and salads and freshly made bread. The guide suggested that I buy some food and use the toilet, as the journey was long and there would probably be no food once we arrived at our destination.

I bought a freshly cooked fish, some rice and another pink drink, which were delicious. Once all the passengers were back on board the boat slowly turned into the tributary. Gradually, it began to empty out as we passed village upon village along the banks of the river. At one particular village, the boat stopped for about an hour. The desks and chairs were untied, and out of nowhere men appeared to carry each piece up the hill to the plateau, and on to the village school. At another village the coal was unloaded, and men with naked torsos and rippling muscles again emerged to carry this rich commodity to the village.

A few kilometres from our destination the sun began to set on the river, and the sky turned a deep red hue that seemed to surround me, taking my breath away. I was so close, and the anticipation and fear that my dream wouldn't turn out as I expected was beginning to consume me. I tried to mentally prepare myself for the unknown, whatever it contained.

Julio appeared on the roof, sitting beside me as the boat chugged its way up river. We were both lost in thought, but after a while he broke the silence.

"This shaman, Don Juanito, is very powerful, but very old. He has been healing people for most of his life and is respected by all the villages around. People come from near and far to be healed by him, and no one has died in his house, which is a great blessing and a sign of power for any *Ayahuasquero*."

"What is an *Ayahuasquero*?" I asked

"That is the name given to shaman who use Ayahuasca as the instrument for healing," he replied.

"How did the Shaman learn to be an *Ayahuasquero*?" I asked, intrigued.

"He was brought up by a tribe of the Bora Bora deep in the Amazon, and began his training when he was eight years old. He was taught in the traditional manner of teacher to apprentice, and had to go through all the rites, rituals, trials and tribulations that are required of a pupil of Ayahuasca." Julio replied.

"Does this tradition of shaman and apprentice still exist?" I asked, feeling my heart beating faster.

"The problem now is that the *metizos* do not have the discipline or courage to undertake such a training. At present Don Juanito is teaching a man called Pepe who lives in one of the villages near by, but there have been some difficulties in the training," Julio replied.

"Really. Like what? " I asked, genuinely interested.

"Pepe believes he has completed his training. He thinks that he is a shaman already. He is taking Ayahuasca and healing without the supervision of Don Juanito, but he is not fully ready."

"What do you mean?"

"Pepe has reached the place where the ego takes control over the heart. The Shaman can no longer be responsible for what will happen to him if he continues to take Ayahuasca without supervision. Now Don Juanito is looking for another person to teach this knowledge to before he dies, one that is strong enough to complete the training," Julio replied, looking straight at me.

"And I am looking for a teacher." I answered, returning Julio's gaze.

"I know this is true, for last night I had a vision of the Shaman and he told me. I know that I am part of something great, leading you to your destiny. You did not come here as a tourist but to find your teacher. If my vision is true I will stay with you for a few days to make sure you are settled with the family, then I will leave you with the Shaman and return to Iquitos." he said in a serious voice.

I looked at the guide and all my doubts about him were washed away. I realised how quick I had been to judge him, and yet he was part of this wonderful adventure and could see the greater plan. My heart gave a leap. I was doing the right thing regardless of the outcome.

"Thank you Julio, I really appreciate your support and respect." I said, genuinely.

"Don't mention it. I am your friend," he answered.

\* \* \*

By the time we reached the Shaman's village the last of the sun's rays were slowly dying into the river and the first stars were already gleaming in the blue-black sky. The full moon was beginning to rise over the river, casting a silver glow on the village, making it look surreal, as though in a living fairy tale. I had arrived.

One kilometre beyond the village the boat docked by two *casitas* that shimmered in the moonlight. Most of the residents live in the village, with a few more families situated further along the bank of the river, including the Shaman's *casita*. We were one of the last people on the boat, and, as I looked around, I was surprised that so many people had been able to fit into such a small space.

In the darkness of the night I saw that the *casitas* were built on stilts about five hundred metres from the river's edge. "Rebecca," Julio called to me. "We have arrived, do you have everything with you?" I grabbed my rucksack and slung it on my back as Julio started to unload all the food and goods I'd bought with me for my stay here. "Come, the Shaman is waiting," he said.

I felt a shiver run down my spine. My heart was pounding and my mouth was dry. At last I was to meet the presence that had been calling me for so long and I was filled with a myriad of emotions; nervousness, excitement, fear and exhilaration. My dream and the vision were about to become real.

The river had shrunk with the onset of the dry season, leaving the riverbank steep and muddy. Gingerly, I stepped off the boat, and clambering up the slippery incline I followed Julio towards the large *casita* that was nearest to the river and built in an L-shape on a clearing about the size of a football pitch, surrounded on all sides by the rainforest. I could see in the darkness the shape of the other *casita* a few metres away. Both were built completely from natural materials, and looked sturdy and strong.

A ladder of about eight steps led into one doorway at the side of the bigger *casita* nearest the river, - which I later learned to be the kitchen - where I noticed the silhouette of a woman squatting on her heels staring at me. At the end of the other section was a larger ladder leading to the longer part of the building, and what looked like the main room of the *casita*. From deep inside came a warm orange glow, cast by a kerosene lamp.

I was led straight to the entrance of this *casita*, and carefully climbed the ladder, with my heart beating fast and my body breaking out in a cold sweat. Thoughts were racing around my head. I suddenly wondered if I had prepared myself enough for this experience. I entered, and looked around in wonder. The room was made of wood, larger than it had looked from the outside, at about thirty metres long, and empty, except for a small table in the far left hand corner. The floor was made from thin slats of wood, and the walls were made of the same type of slats, but they only reached waist height. Trimmed down tree trunks were placed about four metres apart along each side of the room, the spaces between acting as windows. Woven leaves made up the roof, which sloped down, protecting the room from rain. It was the most natural construction I had ever been in, and I immediately felt at home.

The Shaman stood up as I entered the room, and I got to look at him properly for the first time. He was very short, about my height, 5'2" with the facial features of an Amazonian Indian. A smattering of short stubble covered his head, his eyes were deep black, twinkling like stars, and his cheeks were rosy pink in a chocolate-coloured face. He smiled and I could see a mouth full of little stubby teeth. He wore black suit trousers that were so old they looked like rags, and an old white shirt that was now more a shade of grey, through which I could see his hairless chest was stocky, in fact it seemed he had not an ounce of extra weight on him. His skin looked smooth and soft and his hands were incredibly big, wrinkled and scarred with huge gnarled nails. His whole body glowed from the inside. Being so near to this beautiful man I felt a wave of warmth wash over me, and I knew that he was the presence from my visions.

The Shaman disappeared in a sea of his family, who were hovering around patiently waiting to meet the newcomer. Pashco, his wife, came forward first. She had the same ageless quality as the Shaman, the same lines of life defined in her beautiful, regal face. Pashco was also of Indian descent, and her facial features reminded me of a warrior. Dressed in a skirt and torn pink shirt, stained with the sweat of tending the cooking fire, she, like the Shaman, was small and strong, with muscles rippling on her arms and back and legs. Her skin glowed with health, vitality and life.

The Shaman and Pashco had been together for about twenty years, having met in Iquitos while Don Juanito had been an *Ayahuasquero* at the local hospital. Pashco was dying and Don Juanito had cured her illness and fallen in love with her. The

Shaman adopted Pashco's two children, Jovino and Lydia, and they had lived together in Iquitos until the younger son, Jovino, had finished school. The rainforest lived in the spirit of Pashco and the Shaman, and finding Iquitos too civilised, they decided to return to the rainforest, moving to this village on a tributary river.

Jovino was my age and had trained as a teacher, but loved the rainforest life more than life in the city, so was now living in the *casita*. He had survived polio as a child, although it had left him with a deformed left leg that caused him to limp. Jovino was a hunter and fisherman, like most of the young men in the village, and his disability had only given him the determination to prove he was no less able then they. Behind Jovino stood Ramon, a friend of the Shaman's from another village, with his girlfriend Elsa, her newly born baby and her twelve year-old sister, Esther.

I guessed Ramon was in his late thirties but I was not sure, and neither was he. His life story was very sad. His parents, new wife and newly born son had died of a cholera epidemic that had spread through his village. Ramon, having lost his entire family, lost his sanity, and by some good fortune found his way to the Shaman. In return for healing and a place to live, Ramon hunted and provided food for the family. He looked formidable, and at nearly six foot tall towered above us all. Each muscle and sinew was defined in his skeletal form, and he conveyed a hidden fury that scared me. His eyes were always red, which I could only imagine to be psychotic rage at the unfairness of life. I believe that if he had not found the Shaman he would have inflicted a lot of pain on himself, and on anyone unfortunate enough to get on the wrong side of him.

Elsa was eighteen, and had been born in the village. The Shaman was healing her after a jealous *brujo*, or witch, had put a curse on her and her husband while they were living in Iquitos. Fleeing back to the village, Elsa's husband had died from an erupted tumour in his stomach, at the house of another Shaman who could heal neither him nor Elsa. With the baby, and still terrified for her life, she had gone straight to Don Juanito for protection. Here she had met Ramon, and they had started a relationship with the blessing of the Shaman.

Behind this main room, where I was to sleep with Ramon, Elsa, Esther and the baby and any other guests that were visiting, was another smaller room, divided by a partition. This was where Don Juanito, Pashco and Jovino slept. Jutting out towards the river was the kitchen. There was no wall at the end of the kitchen, just a big gap overlooking the river. This was the area where the food was prepared and cooked over an open fire, with the waste thrown out for the five dogs, the chickens, and whatever animal happened to be living there at that time. There was another ladder leading to the kitchen, and this was where Pashco had been squatting when I first arrived.

Fifty metres from the house, on the same patch of land, stood another, smaller *casita*, where Pashco's daughter, thirty-two year old Lydia, lived with her husband Walter and their two children, Eric and Doily. The two families shared food and all other resources, which included two shotguns, four canoes, and two *chakras* (gardens for cultivating vegetables, fruit and yucca).

Directly behind the two *casitas* the rainforest began, and in front of them the river flowed into the Amazon. The river was now the source of life for me. I would wash myself in it every morning and evening, clean clothes in it, cook with it and drink it. It was also our main source of food. The river was famous for its variety of deliciously exotic fish.

After all the introductions had been made everyone seemed to disappear, and I was left alone. Sitting on the floor, waiting patiently was the Shaman. His back was against the wall and the kerosene lamp was burning on the table in the corner, throwing an orange glow across the room and casting shadows on the opposite wall. He was playing with his pipe with his big gnarled hands, and looked up as I approached. I sat down opposite him and felt the whole world stand still. The rainforest noises receded into the distance and everything seemed to be holding its breath in anticipation.

The Shaman looked up at me, and I saw a face etched with the experience of life. He did not say a word, but took my hand and looked deep into my eyes. For an eternity, his eyes bored into mine. I felt him exploring my deepest secrets and seeing my life's journey to this moment.

Suddenly, his face broke into a huge smile. "Welcome Rebekita, you are the one I have been waiting for," he said. "I heard your heart's request and called to you. Now you will stay some time and learn with me. You have come to learn the art of living, and the art of healing. I see you have travelled far in your life, searching, and have found many answers. Do you know how you found me?" asked the Shaman.

"I had a vision of you, and felt you calling me, then things happened beyond my control to lead me to you," I answered.

"No, Rebekita, this is not how you found me. Many people have visions and dreams but they do not find them. Why do you think so many people do not find their dreams?"

"I don't know, I guess many people do not have the courage to follow something as intangible, as unreal as dreams."

"Exactly. The reason you found me was because you believed in the dream. You believed it could be a reality. You had total faith in finding me."

"I'm not sure I understand, Don Juanito, lots of people have faith, but they still do not realise their dreams," I protested.

"Ahhh, this is the right question. The reason these people do not find their dreams is because even though they believe, they also have doubt in their heart. Even an ounce of doubt in the dream will never make it a reality."

"But I had doubt, and I still found you," I said, confused.

"If you examine your journey closely, Rebekita, you will see that you did not doubt the dream. You doubted whether you would find it in Peru. You did not doubt me, or whether I existed. You doubted whether I would live up to your expectations. You always believed in the dream, your doubt came from your expectations and wants," answered the Shaman.

"You mean that all dreams come true when you have absolutely no doubt that it can become a reality?" I asked, seeing the process so clearly, now that I had arrived.

"That is some of it. You did not give up searching for me, even when you thought it was crazy, and others doubted."

"In other words, I created my own reality."

"Yes, and more importantly, you are beginning to realise your true power, the power that is within every human being. Everyone must follow their heart in order to find out who they truly are."

"But there is so much fear and confusion that most people do not know how to listen to their hearts."

"First one must learn faith, courage, strength and conviction, the tools needed to follow the heart. Only then can real happiness be experienced."

"What is real happiness, Don Juanito?"

The Shaman looked me directly in the eyes, and I felt them touch my heart. "Real happiness, Rebekita, is unconditional love for who you are. You have found me because you are ready to understand what that means. The Amazonian plant, the *Mother of all Medicine*, Ayahuasca, will teach you to love and accept yourself. But first you must go deep within to heal your own pain and suffering. True shaman first learn to heal themselves before they can heal others. This is Ayahuasca's gift."

Before I could ask him another question he took my other hand in his, and spoke in a tone that came from the depths of his power, as a shaman and teacher, which resonated at the very core of my being. "Now I must ask you, Rebekita, this is a difficult path you have decided to tread, and many who have attempted to have gone mad. This is not a journey for the weak and fearful.

# THE SHAMAN AND HIS APPRENTICE

You will see many things that will frighten you, visions of spirits, serpents and all kinds of weird and terrifying animals that will seem very real. Most frightening of all you will face yourself. Are you ready to face yourself, in all your glory and all your malevolence, and become the Shaman's apprentice?"

"Yes, I am ready," I managed to whisper, without any doubt. I was ready to do whatever I had to, in order to find myself.

## PART TWO – EXPLORATION

*What happens when your soul*
*Begins to awaken*
*Your eyes*
*And your heart*
*And the cells of your body*
*To the great Journey of Love?*

Hafiz
Sufi Mystic

## CHAPTER FIVE

## *Jungle Lessons*

After three days Julio decided to go back to Iquitos. It was evident I was here to learn under the tutelage of the Shaman, and so no longer required his services as a guide, although it had been good to have him with me. He had helped me to become accustomed to this new way of life, by being able to understand my Western fears and explaining everything in English. On Sunday morning he left early, and I was on my own with the Shaman for the first time. As I waved Julio off it struck me that there was no going back. The apprenticeship could really begin.

That afternoon, and every Sunday, was the one day in the week that villagers gathered together to play football, drink, play cards and generally enjoy themselves, forgetting for a day the challenges of living in the rainforest. It was a beautiful sunny afternoon, and there was a cool breeze blowing as Don Juanito, Walter, Eric, Doily and I walked the kilometre to the village to watch the weekly football game. I had already seen the village from the boat, but now there was the opportunity to meet the inhabitants and learn something about the life they led.

When we arrived the men had already begun to play football, and most of the villagers were either watching from the balcony of the village shop, or from the *casitas* on stilts dotted around the perimeter of the pitch. Don Juanito and I climbed the steps and entered the village shop. He immediately made his way to a group of aged men playing cards, and sat down as they greeted him with laughter and smiles. A bottle of beer and some loose change was all he needed to be included in the game.

I smiled at Don Juanito's happy face, and wandered onto the balcony to watch the match. From this vantage point everyone seemed content and relaxed. Some of the children were playing volleyball, or climbing on the apparatus outside the school, while Eric and his friends were playing their own version of soccer. The women gathered on the benches below, to discuss the weekly gossip, the old men in the village shop were drinking cold beer and playing cards, and the young men were playing what looked like a very violent football game. Most of them were shirtless and shoeless, yet they all had excellent ball control, and were taking the match very seriously.

The game was exciting, and Jovino, the Shaman's son, won the match by scoring in the last minute, which aroused a cheer from the onlookers. As I looked down he looked up, caught my eye, and gave me a little wave. I waved back, feeling the warm glow of recognition ease my fears of isolation. Despite the promise I had made that I would let go of my Western upbringing and conditioning, and endeavour to integrate myself completely into rainforest life, I wondered whether I would ever really fit in.

I walked back inside, where Don Juanito was waiting for me. I commented how cheerful everyone looked. The Shaman looked at me in surprise. "That's because it's Sunday. Come Rebekita," he said before I could say anything else, "we have to buy some supplies from the shop before we leave."

Each village along the banks of the river has a shop that sells the necessities needed to make life easier in the rainforest. Utilities such as batteries for torches, toilet paper, kerosene for the oil lamps, salt for cooking, and matches to light the fire, are important commodities in the rainforest. Some people are too poor even to have these things, and luxuries such as sugar, rice, and coffee are goods most people cannot afford. The Shaman's family were grateful that I had brought so much with me.

About ten houses surrounded the big football pitch, and after the game we stayed in the village, so that Don Juanito could introduce me to the families that lived in this rural community. Everyone was very friendly and inviting, curious to meet the 'gringa' who had just arrived, and we were offered plenty of food and drink.

At the far end of the plateau stood the school and the Care International charity hut. Don Juanito showed me around the school, which had only recently been reopened. When the river swells it covers the entire plateau and floods the village. The school has to close for about three months, because the rains cause the river to rise higher than the stilts it is built on. During the rainy season the village is deserted, as families move into the heart of the rainforest, and the only means of travel is by canoe.

When the Shaman and Pashco first moved to the village they thoroughly explored the surrounding area, until they found a piece of land deep in the rainforest away from the flooding river. Here they planted two large *chakras* where they sowed yucca, pineapple, root potatoes, maize, watermelon and rainforest vegetables. They also built three casitas, one for Walter, Lydia and the children, and one for the Shaman, Pashco and Jovino, the third being used as the communal kitchen and eating area. They called the place, *'El Centro'* and it was periodically used as a holiday home during the dry season in order to maintain the *chakras*.

When we arrived back at the house the sun was beginning to set, giving the river a wonderful hazy quality. The sounds of the rainforest seemed to be amplified, and the colour of the sky was a rich mixture of yellows, pinks, blues and reds. Far above us twinkled the first stars of dusk, and a slight breeze blew through the *casita. Funny that*, I thought as I looked out at the dying sun and breathed the pure, cool air, *despite coming from a society that considers itself so advanced, I feel a calm here that I have never felt in the West.* As I took another deep breath I became aware of a peaceful contentment within me that filled my whole body.

The Shaman and I sat on the steps looking out over the river at the approaching night. I was comfortable in the silence between us, lost in my thoughts. My mind was running at top speed, and I eventually voiced some of my questions. "Don Juanito, it seems as if education is not really considered important, and yet if the children do not receive a full education how can they ever have the chance to find employment and better themselves?" I asked.

"In the rainforest, lessons of survival, such as hunting and fishing, are considered as important and educational as school. Here having enough food to eat is essential for survival," the Shaman answered.

"But why do people find it so easy to accept the discomforts and difficulties of living here?" I asked.

"Here in the rainforest we live in harmony with nature. Only by living in harmony can we be truly happy, whether in the rainforest or in the city, regardless of the material possessions we have."

"But everyone seems so content with what they have. Why do they not strive for something better?"

"In the rainforest everyone is equal. Everyone helps each other. No family is ever alone or isolated, and there is always support and help available. In the Amazon we have everything we need. Nature supplies us with all the materials and food that we desire, and we do not need to buy many things. Money only has a limited use here. Every day is a fight for survival, to eat, so it is important to be a good hunter or fisherman. There are no banks or moneylenders here in the *selva*," he answered.

We lapsed into silence as I tried to absorb what it meant to live in a world where there were no financial commitments, and no one was a slave to debt, to overdrafts, to credit cards, or to loans. I suddenly received a flash of inspiration.

"In the West, our financial systems teach us to fear money by manipulating us to save for a future that has yet to exist. With our thoughts permanently fixed on the future we are constantly living in fear of the unknown," I continued as my thoughts began to crystallise.

"Rebekita, that is the most fundamental difference between the rainforest and the West"

"What is, Don Juanito?"

"Because money has become the focus of life in your country, many are not following the path that will make them happy. Rebekita, we all have a guiding voice within that leads us through life. These guiding voices are our dreams, messages, and visions. The need to make money stops people from following their dreams. Then people get sick."

"Don Juanito, are you saying that illness is directly related to not listening to our guiding voice?" I replied excitedly.

"Yes, that is exactly what I am saying. Disease is only a lack of balance in the body. Disease comes when a person fails to listen to their calling."

"What do you mean?"

"Disease is only really a wake up call to start living."

"I don't understand."

"Well, you see Rebekita, when we are attached to illnesses we only focus on the disease. We forget to see life as a journey where everything is flowing and in motion, so that illness and disease are actually opportunities for growth."

"I'm still not sure I understand."

"Disease is the spirit's way of expressing that it is unhappy and in pain, and that it can no longer be ignored. Most people become distressed by illness, and this only increases the suffering because our fear of death causes us to fear disease. We have been taught to believe that death is punishment, and if we are good people we will not get sick, or we will be cured. It is time we start to embrace death and accept it as part of the inevitable experience of life. Illness is a chance to make life changes, to start really living. It gives us the opportunity to remember what is important in our lives, to follow our dreams, to heal old wounds and say goodbye. Illness empowers the spirit to be heard and to show the way to a more fulfilling life, for however long that is." As he was speaking I was reminded of the woman with cancer who had come into my shop that sunny spring morning. It was becoming clear to me that we cannot fight disease or illness, but must see it as part of the journey of life and use it as an opportunity to heal ourselves on deeper levels.

"So why is it different here in the rainforest?" I asked.

"People come to a shaman because they are looking to heal the cause of the sickness and not the symptom," the Shaman answered.

"So what does a shaman do then? Does the shaman heal the disease?" I asked, intrigued.

"No Rebekita," the Shaman replied impatiently. "Only the patient can heal their disease, no one else, and even then, what does it mean to heal? Even when you are sick you can still be healed."

"That doesn't make sense," I argued. "How can you still be sick, and be healed at the same time?" I protested.

"When we are truly happy with our life and with everything in it, and when we can see that everything is love, only then are we healed, regardless of whether our bodies are dying."

"Can Ayahuasca help?" I asked.

"Yes, because Ayahausaca teaches us how to truly love who we are, and once we have learnt to love ourselves disease of the spirit can no longer exist."

"How can a plant teach us to love ourselves?" I asked in disbelief.

"Ayahuasca shows us our deepest fears, thus allowing us to accept ourselves."

"How?" I insisted.

"Patience Rebekita, all will be revealed in good time. You want to know everything now, but with patience you can learn by experience, and that is true wisdom," the Shaman said, putting an end to the conversation.

We were silent for a long while, staring out into the indigo sky and listening to the night sounds of the rainforest. The last canoe had passed by, and everything was still and peaceful on the river. Suddenly the Shaman broke the silence between us. In a very serious voice he said, "Rebekita you are preparing to embark on a vision quest. This is the journey to the self and you can take no personal belongings with you. Nobody can help you, no one can save you and nobody can guide you. Any illusions you have of yourself, any grand images, will be broken down and shattered. Beware Rebekita, many people have walked this path and gone mad, others have lost their confidence and their sense of self. This is not a journey for the faint-hearted. This is the battle between light and dark, the ego and the heart, love and fear, life and death. But now it is time for bed. Tomorrow we have a busy day, as you will join us on the hunt, and it can be very tiring. Sleep well, we will speak more tomorrow."

\* \* \*

I awoke early after a restless night, eager with anticipation. I knew it was a great honour to be invited to join the hunt, for this was a male activity that women rarely participated in. I dressed underneath my mosquito net, and quietly stepped out onto the veranda. The rainforest was quiet, and the east was glowing a light blue in contrast with the darkness of the rest of the sky. There was no moon, and the stars still twinkled in the depths of space. The river was shrouded in mist as I washed, the cold water clearing my head.

Pashco was already up and organising breakfast by the time I climbed up the ladder to the kitchen. The fire was lit and burning brightly, while the eastern sky glowed an orange and pink hue as the sun began its travels across the Amazon. The Shaman was sitting at his favourite place by the open window, watching the rising sun. The smell of fish soup reached my nose, and I realised how hungry I was.

Sitting down beside him we watched the sun make its slow ascent to heaven whilst waiting for breakfast.

"So Rebekita, you seem quiet this morning. Is something on your mind?" The Shaman said, turning towards me.

"Actually there is, it is about the hunt. It conflicts with my belief that humans should not eat animals. I have been a vegetarian for many years because the thought of killing any living animal for food repulses me. I'm having to prepare myself emotionally." I replied.

On hearing that the Shaman began to roar with laughter.

"In the rainforest, if you cannot hunt you do not eat." the Shaman stated. "You have much choice in your country, your shops have all the food you could want, but here in the rainforest we have to rely on nature for survival. A good hunter is a good husband. My family is blessed because we have dogs to help us hunt, and guns to shoot monkeys and birds."

"Why are dogs so important to the hunt?" I enquired.

"Dogs can smell prey hidden from sight that humans are unable to detect. A hunt is almost always successful when you have dogs. Some hunters cannot afford dogs and guns, and still use the traditional methods of killing."

"What are the those ways, and why don't you use them anymore?" I asked.

"Nowadays people are lazy and it is easier to kill with dogs and guns, as you will see today. I will show you how to kill using the old ways, later. But remember Rebekita, it isn't the form of killing that is important. It is to remember that we all belong to this earth. For every wild pig, monkey or other animal we kill, there is one less animal to eat. Hunting teaches us how animals and humans rely on each other for survival. For it is not the act of killing that is important, it is the intention of the hunter. Intention is the key to every action. If you kill with respect, then the animal dies not in vain, but by giving its life for food. A wise hunter knows never to kill more than he needs to feed his family."

"I still do not understand completely. How does an animal know if it is killed with right intention?"

"Aahh Rebekita, you underestimate the animal world. Every animal feels fear, and every animal hunts for its food."

"Exactly, but they don't hunt us, so surely humans control animals," I asked.

"Huh," the Shaman snorted. "You Western people, so full of arrogance. Humans are not ever in control because every living thing is a part of nature – the cycles of life. As I said, the key is to balance these cycles, so we only kill enough to eat. I think in your society it is more of a business and even has financial gain attached to it. Yes?"

"This is the very reason why I am vegetarian. In the West we are spending excessive amounts of money, and vital resources like land and water, on the 'meat business'. So many unnecessary animals are slaughtered to feed our greed, while people all over the world die of malnutrition every day."

"Exactly, in your Western world, animals are killed indiscriminately, their meat is wasted and their soul does not understand why it has died. This is the crime of a society that has lost its connection with the animal kingdom. None is greater than the other for we all have our part to play in the cycles of life. When an animal is killed for greed the animal dies in fear, and then the human consumes all the energy of the fear and can become sick themselves."

I thought of all our recent meat scares, BSE, CJD, and foot and mouth, the hormones we use to make animals grow quicker in order to feed our need to have more than we could ever consume. Maybe our greed had even greater implications then we realised.

I looked up at the Shaman still full of questions, but could see from his expression that the conversation had ended. He looked into my troubled face and sighed.

"Rebekita, always so many questions. You do not need to understand anymore, now you must learn from experience, then you will be a great hunter. Now we must concentrate on calling the animals to us, to give up their lives for our food, and remember, we always kill in the right spirit, always with the right intention."

\* \* \*

The hunt consisted of Don Juanito, Jovino, Ramon, Walter, myself, and the five dogs. Don Juanito led us through a trail into the rainforest. The dogs followed until we were deep in the jungle, and then they disappeared into the thick foliage, leaping and jumping over the tree roots and small bushes. The hunters separated and spread out in different directions, carrying axes, machetes or guns. I followed the Shaman, ducking under lianas, and stepping over fallen logs as he cut us a path with his machete. We soon came upon a fallen tree trunk, and handing me a cigarette we sat in silence and had a smoke. Just as we finished, we heard barking and howling coming from far away. "That's Omega, calling the hunters to the prey. Better go and see what the dog has caught," said the Shaman. Jumping off the log, he led us unerringly towards Omega's barking. We broke through a clearing, and there were the dogs, jumping and clawing at the old hollow trunk of a fallen tree.

The tree was rotten and hollow, a safe place for animals to hide. Inside this particular log the dogs had found an anteater snuggled safely in its depths, and were clawing at the outer bark, but it was too tough. Walter and Jovino stood at one end of the trunk, and Don Juanito stood at the other end. Already Ramon had begun to chop away at the middle of the tree trunk with the axe. The tree bark was very thick and it took real brute strength to hack away at it. While Ramon was busy with this, Walter and Jovino began to enlarge the hole in order to push the anteater further into the trunk, as Don Juanito stood at the other end, just in case it tried to escape from there. The whole event seemed to take forever as the hunters chopped away at the fallen tree and the dogs barked and howled, leaping across the trunk, as if urging the hunters on. The animal seemed safe and secure in its deep dark depths and I wondered if we would ever reach it. At last Ramon, shirtless, hot and sweaty with his muscles rippling, broke through the middle of the trunk forcing the anteater to try to escape.

The dogs went crazy as we spotted the animal for the first time, trying to reach one of the openings the hunters had made. Walter was waiting for it with the machete, and I watched in horror as he attacked this poor, defenceless creature with one vicious swipe of the machete, as it made its last attempt at freedom. The animal screamed with pain and fear, collapsing by the hunter's feet but refusing to die, even after the second blow.

Ramon strode over, took the axe and repeatedly smashed the top of the anteater's head until the animal's shrieks became moans and then were silenced altogether. I felt sick to the core as he ended the life of the anteater, and turned away, trying not to cry.

The dogs finally stopped their barking, and the whole forest seemed silent and restful after the nervous energy of the hunt. I wiped away some tears before anyone could see. However, Ramon was looking at me intently, and smiling said, "Look at the *gringa*, crying over this animal. She will not be crying with hunger for the next three days 'though." The others laughed, and despite feeling humiliated I knew he was right. For the first time in my life I felt that I had the right to eat meat, for I had been part of the process of hunting and killing. Working as a team, each hunter had an integral part to play. The animal's need to survive was as powerful as ours was for eating it. The smell of blood and death, as well as the energy, time and effort it took to hunt the anteater would put most people off eating meat ever again.

We strung the anteater on some sticks tied with twine from a shredded rainforest branch, and walked towards home with our prize. Pashco and Elsa were waiting for us at the *casitas* with the fire ablaze. The first thing they did was put the animal on the flames to singe the fur, in order to pluck it easily. Once all the fur was removed the carcass was taken to the river, cleaned thoroughly, and gutted. The eatable organs and the meat were taken back to the kitchen, and the uneatable parts of the anteater were left near the river for the wild animals.

In the kitchen, the meat was cut up into cubes and placed into a big saucepan of water, for meat soup, to be served with rice and *platano*. The organs were fried lightly and given to the dogs, as a reward for their hard work. There was plenty to go round and nothing was wasted. Every part of the anteater had been utilised for human or animal consumption.

During the preparation of the meat, Don Juanito took me aside. "Let's go, while no one is looking." I turned to him in relief, the smell and sight of blood and dead meat was making my stomach turn. We sneaked out undetected and followed the same trail back into the rainforest. The Shaman took me onto a different path and we were soon heading towards the sun. As we went further into the jungle we heard noises above us. Gazing up we could see monkeys playing in the trees.

Looking around, the Shaman spotted a plant that was poisonous to monkeys, and began to sharpen its tip with his machete, turning it into a dart. Cutting another plant that had a hollow stem, he placed one end of the stalk to his mouth and improvised how a traditional hunter would blow the dart through the stalk, expertly hitting the monkey in a certain part of its body.

"An accomplished and skilled hunter could hit a monkey up in the treetops, killing it almost instantly, and silently, so that the other animals were unaware," said the Shaman in a reverent voice. "Killing in silence is important. If you kill with a loud gun, the animals never come back; the monkeys will find other trees to play in. If you kill with indiscriminate greed a mother pig, which is the biggest and fattest, the young piglets cannot survive, thus reducing the amount of food provided by the pack. Accomplished and trained hunters realised that hunting was a strategic undertaking that kept the cycles of life flowing and only killing what was needed, to ensure a regular food supply."

Not all my questions had been answered, but I was getting a clearer idea of how our lives are so interwoven with the natural world. Amidst the confusion and the shouting, the sound of axe hitting wood, the scurrying of dogs digging their way into the trunk, and the killing of the anteater, the cycles of life were being completed. I was looking forward to my first meat soup in over twenty years.

\* \* \*

A few days later I awoke early, just as the eastern sky was glowing pink, and walked into the kitchen. The Shaman, Jovino and Ramon had already left to go fishing, and Pashco was re-stoking the fire. She looked up and nodded to me in greeting as I entered. As she placed a steaming cup of coffee in front of me, and sat down opposite, I felt a warmth from her I had not previously experienced. "Today, Rebekita, we are preparing *masato*, nectar of the rainforest. It is a drink made from yucca. We will need to go to the *chakra* to harvest it, as we will need a lot. You will help to prepare it?" I nodded in agreement.

"In the time of my grandmother, women who had their monthly bleeding were prohibited from preparing *masato*, now only women who are unwell mentally or physically are not allowed to make it." Pashco said.

I was puzzled by what she was saying. "But Pashco, why, what is wrong with women who are menstruating?"

Pashco became silent and her eyes took on a far away look. After a short time she turned to face me. "In modern times women have forgotten what it means to have their monthly bleeding. Where I come from it was considered an auspicious time for women, a time when they reconnected with themselves and Mother Earth. It was a time for rest, and to re-energise. This was when women gave thanks for the blood that binds life and death together and purifies a woman's body from the growth of life that was not meant to be. Menstruation blood was also used to heal a number of specific feminine ailments. Over time the special relationship that women have with Mother Earth has almost been forgotten. Rites and rituals that balanced and gave meaning to a woman's life and connected her to her real purpose on this earth - to enable the evolution and growth of our children - have not been passed on from mother to daughter and are almost lost.

This purpose cannot be underestimated, and yet women all over the world have chosen to ignore this path. Even here, some women, like Elsa, leave the rainforest to go to Iquitos to make money, but most of them return to the rainforest where life is hard, but more simple to understand."

We sipped our coffee in amicable silence both lost in our thoughts. "Pashco," I said breaking the silence, "in my country women have fought hard for their freedom, yet in our strivings to become self-sufficient, and in order to fit into the system, we have been unable to nurture our feminine qualities, or be truly honoured and respected as mothers for the next generation."

"Ah, Rebekita, we cannot wait for the system to change. It is up to the individual, man and woman, to make this choice. Each person needs to make the decision. What is more important, values based on love or values based on money? Only if the majority choose love will we see a future where we are all truly free," Pashco replied.

"Come, it is getting late," she said, changing the subject before I could ask her any more questions. We finished our coffee and made the short way to the *chakra* at the back of the *casita*. The *chakra* was about the size of a football pitch, and filled with vegetables and fruit. It had been made just before I arrived, a long process that consisted of cutting down the trees and then burning the area, making the soil fertile.

Many people from the West see the burning of large areas of rainforest by the village people as being destructive, but this couldn't be further from the truth. As I observed in the hunt, the rainforest people work in harmony with nature, and their way of life is in tune with the cycles of the earth, which guarantees the continuation of their own existence. When we killed the animal every part of it was utilised, eventually finding its way back into the soil, thus completing the cycle. Likewise, rainforest people cultivate the land to produce enough food to feed their families until the soil is exhausted, and then they abandon it to nature. The rainforest rejuvenates at an incredibly rapid pace and within a few years there is no sign that there was ever a clearing, the soil and vegetation becoming as lush and fertile as ever.

The sun was beginning to rise, and even though it was still a cool morning, it promised to be another hot day. Pashco showed me the plantation and handed me a sack. I was given orders to collect about thirty yucca plants. Pashco knelt down in the mud and showed me how to pull them out of the ground. Yucca is a root vegetable that looks like a parsnip, and is yellow in colour with a brownish type bark around it. Filled with minerals and nutrients, it is the main staple of the rainforest diet. It can be fried, boiled, fermented to make an alcoholic beverage, or made into *masato*, which was often considered a meal in itself.

After about two hours of digging, Pashco and I had about

thirty pieces of yucca each. The sun was high in the sky and we were both red and sweating. Pashco helped me to lift the sack onto my back, and together we lumbered through the rainforest to the *casita*, the trees cooling my burning head. I threw the sack on the kitchen floor, breathing a sigh of relief as I sank to my knees in the welcoming shade. My back was aching, and I was dirty and tired. "Don't worry Rebekita, once you taste *masato* you will know it was worth it," Pachco said when she saw the state I was in.

As we rested, Elsa, who had not been able to help us in the *chakra* because of her illness, cut up a few of the small round yellow lemons that were grown there, and squeezed them into sugared water to cool us down. After we had rested Pashco emptied the sacks onto the floor and together we started shelling the yucca. Unlike parsnip skins that are scraped off using a peeler, yucca has a strong bark around it that needs to be peeled off using a knife or machete. Lydia and Doily entered the kitchen with another sack of the vegetable, and together the four of us shelled the mountain of yucca before us, while Elsa prepared the fire.

When all the yuccas were peeled, we chopped them up into thick, chunky pieces, put them into a big cauldron of boiling water, and cooked them to a soft mush. Draining the remaining water out of the pot, Pashco poured the yucca pieces into a specially prepared *masato* dish. About two metres long and one metre deep, the dish was like a mini canoe made of wood, which we all sat around while waiting for the soft mountain of yellow mush to cool down. A spoon was handed to each of us, but not knowing why, I wondered what would come next.

Pashco took a spoonful of the yucca mush. Blowing to cool it down, she then swirled it around her mouth for about twenty seconds. Once it was well and truly masticated and mixed with saliva, she spat it back into the *masato* canoe. Doily, Elsa, Pashco and Lydia had been waiting patiently for my reaction, and I didn't disappoint them. I looked in shock and then horror. That was disgusting and animalistic! The thought of having to share my saliva with these rainforest women made me feel physically sick. In London, I didn't even drink from the same glass as another person, or share the same cutlery. My immediate thought was to refuse to participate any further in the preparation.

But somehow I knew this was a test. The time had come to let go of my inbuilt paranoia regarding sanitation and cleanliness if I wanted to be able to enjoy myself with these women, and be accepted by them. Solicitously, I took a spoonful of the mush, as the women watched me eagerly. I wanted to retch, but instead tried not to think about what I was doing, numbly swirling the mouthful of yucca around my mouth. Once it was masticated, I copied Pashco by spitting it into the canoe, globules of yucca running down my chin. The women clapped, and together each sprayed a mouthful of yucca into the canoe.

Here were grown women spraying out huge globs of yucca saturated with spittle! Seeing the funny side of it, I got the giggles, which became infectious and soon we were all laughing hysterically. This conduct would be considered offensive in the West, because we are so blinded by what we are conditioned to believe. For these women, there was no judgement, only an acceptance that this was part of the process for making *masato*. Once Pashco had explained to me that saliva released enzymes in the yucca that make it creamy and thick, I realised how limiting my conditioning had been. After the first few spoonfuls I soon started to really enjoy myself. I felt a sense of freedom. I also saw the sharing of my saliva as a kind of initiation, and felt that I could now be accepted as part of the family.

It took a good few hours to masticate the entire 'yucca canoe'. While Pashco slowly added water until the mixture became creamy in consistency, we chatted, gossiping about the other people from the village, telling stories and talking through various problems. Making *masato* is an important social ritual for rainforest women. It provides a space and time for women to get together and relax, in a week that is often filled with isolated stress and hard physical work. There was a lot of laughter during the making of *masato*, and that element alone made the preparation of it something I looked forward to.

After the *masato* was finished Lydia and Doily went back to their house, while Pashco and I waited patiently for Jovino, Ramon and Don Juanito to return. It was nearly noon and the men would be bringing our lunch. I decided to take the opportunity to ask Pashco what she meant about mental and physical states of mind, and how this could affect the taste of *masato*. Pashco sat silently for some time looking at me. "When a person cooks, their energy is automatically transferred to the food," she finally replied.

"But how can that be?"

"Every living thing on this earth is just a ball of vibrating energy, which is both negative and positive. A person is one or the other depending on what is happening to them, inside their soul. If a person is angry the neutral energy of the food is affected and becomes an angry vibration. Likewise, if a person is happy and prepares the food with love, it vibrates with love."

"But how can you taste the difference?" I asked.

"That's the easy part. Once you are aware of your own vibrations it is easy to taste the vibrations of others."

"You mean that if I eat food prepared by an angry person, then I absorb their anger?"

"Yes, and it doesn't only extend to food. It is also in every physical and mental contact you have with another person. If you spend a lot of time around a person with negative energy, their emotions can often be so over powering that you start vibrating negativity too."

"What is negative energy?" I asked.

"Fear, and all things that come from fear, such as anger, frustration, hate, loathing, pain, sadness, despair, resentment, and regret."

"So I can feel these emotions just by being around negative people, because I have absorbed their energy." I clarified. Pashco nodded.

This was what the Shaman had meant when he said that we digest the fear of the animal that is being slaughtered. He meant the energy of the animal at the moment of its death was automatically transferred to the eater. I thought of all the animals that are so cruelly slaughtered, and shivered involuntarily. I was relieved I had been a vegetarian for so long.

Pashco interrupted my thoughts. "Yes, but the opposite is true too, when you surround yourself with positive energy."

"What is positive energy?"

"The only positive energy that truly exists, Rebekita, is love. And the greatest expression of that is loving yourself."

"What do you mean?"

"The first step in learning to love ourselves is to surround ourselves with loving energy. Food is a vital part of the process because we are taking in sustenance. The more love we surround ourselves with, the more we become aware of negative energy, and realise that it does not serve happiness".

We lapsed into silence. It was true that when I had reached the pit of my depression before my suicide attempt, everything around me was dark and negative too. Even now, most of the news and programmes on television and radio only seemed to focus on images and stories that were depressing. Were these forms of communication only reflecting what the majority of people were feeling inside? If this was the case the world was indeed becoming a sick place.

However, if Pashco was saying that the world was only a reflection of my own mood, maybe I could reflect a different reality, one that was filled with positive energy. Did that mean I could create a world filled with love and light? This thought scared me. Was I really that powerful? I suddenly felt a strong impatient desire to take Ayahuasca. Only Ayahuasca could open my subconscious and help me understand myself enough to choose to see the world in another way.

A call from the river broke my reverie. Don Juanito, Jovino and Ramon had arrived, the canoe filled with enough fish to feed both families for the next two days. We called back in greeting, and went down to the riverbank to help carry the buckets of fish to the kitchen. Then we all sat around and drank the *masato*. It tasted like nectar, and became my favourite rainforest drink. After my discussion with Pashco, I was sure it tasted that good because the family always prepared it with love.

## CHAPTER SIX

## *Witches and Shaman*

I sat by the edge of the river as the sun slowly disappeared, leaving behind a trail of yellow, gold and red. The sounds of the night creatures broke the stillness, a cool breeze rustled through the trees, and I shivered despite the lingering warmth of the day. My mind, usually racing with thoughts, was slowing down. I had been in the rainforest for a while, and things were now becoming familiar.

I had fallen into the routine easily, and enjoyed the slow pace of the rainforest. Time, as I had known it, no longer existed. Here, minutes could often feel like hours, and because everything was so new and different, some days felt like an eternity, while others sped past. However, things were getting simpler. I now felt comfortable with the food, the heat and humidity, the smells, the long days and even longer nights, and the incessant mosquitoes.

The daily routine consisted of waking at first light to go down to the river's edge to bathe, before the river became busy with fishermen and hunters. As the sun rises above the trees, the rainforest comes alive with sounds of monkeys, birds and the other millions of species that dwell in the ancient Amazon. After washing, the Shaman and I would sip sweet coffee, while Pashco prepared the fire. The Shaman, Jovino (when he was around), Pashco, Ramon, Elsa, Esther and I always ate breakfast a couple of hours after dawn. This was usually leftovers from the night before, and could be fish soup, meat soup (*wangana, rat, mordello, anuje,* or *majass*) or as a rare treat, fried sweet bananas. Sometimes Ramon would fish during the night or very early in the morning, so that we would have fresh fish soup instead.

After breakfast our day varied, according to our whims, and whether we had enough food or not. Don Juanito and I would go fishing, explore the rainforest, or potter around in the chakra. Everything was grown without the use of pesticides, and there was a constant need to cultivate and inspect our fruit and vegetables. One of the most important jobs was looking for worms that hid under the leaves.

I was fortunate enough to be in the rainforest during the watermelon season, when they would grow big, red and juicy. This lasts for about one month, and we would walk to the watermelon plantation after breakfast, and choose a watermelon each. Carrying these back to the house, we would sit under the cool shade eating the rich, sweet flesh.

Lunch was eaten after the main activity for the day had been completed. The afternoon was spent in our hammocks, walking in the rainforest, or just sitting in silence. With no television, music, telephones, books, radio or external distractions of any kind, I was finding it hard to be still. My mind, not used to the lack of stimulation and noise, would often become restless and doubtful.

When this occurred the Shaman would somehow sense it and suggest a walk, or start talking with me, or play the *Shakira* tape I had given him, and the feelings would evaporate.

It was the nights that were the most difficult times. We were usually in our *mosquiteros* an hour or two after the sun had disappeared, sometimes earlier if the mosquitoes were vicious. Under the *mosquitero*, isolated from the world, I would lie awake for hours, trying to analyse and construct a rational understanding for what I was experiencing. This often led to equal amounts of wonder and disbelief at what was happening to me.

The main focus of life in the Amazon is to ensure there is a constant food supply, and the chores seem to be equally shared by both men and women. Women look after the children, fish, collect firewood, carry the water from the river to the house, cultivate the *chakra*, and sow vegetables, fruits, and yucca. Men hunt, fish, chop firewood, build and cultivate *chakras*, and construct *casitas*.

My family were proficient fishermen, and never failed to make some impressive catches, including *Oscar fish, peacock bass, Sanguro, arawana, piranha, catfish,* and a variety of other colourful and unusually adapted tropical fish. Occasionally, Ramon, Don Juanito, Jovino and Walter would go on a fishing expedition and camp by the Oxbow Lakes, returning the next day. Pashco, Lydia, Doily, Elsa and I would wait for them in the morning with the fire burning. It was always chaos when the catch came in. Buckets of slimy, jumping fish would be hauled up the bank to the kitchen, and the rest of our morning consisted of cleaning and gutting the catch, while the men relaxed in the shade and smoked, regaling us with their tales.

The first few times the catch came in I felt really nauseous and ill at the smell of blood, slime and scales, and I always refused to help. Then, one day, while I sat in the kitchen watching the chaos around me, resisting the smell and sight of fish, I realised I was missing out on an experience. I had overcome my barriers with *masato*, now it was time to do the same here. Grabbing my machete without allowing another thought to stop me, I took a fish from the bucket and started to scrape the scales off its slimy body. Looking up, Pashco smiled to me and nodded her head. I smiled back. I was starting to let go.

Every so often, I was reminded of the dangers of living in the rainforest. One morning, while we were eating, Pashco grabbed her machete and started smashing it around the breakfast plates.

I looked on bemused, thinking she must've gone mad, when a streak of grey dashed across the dishes. My look turned to horror as a huge, furry tarantula spider headed straight for me. As quick as a flash, Pashco sliced it in two before it could reach me, and it fell through a crack in the floorboards. "Be careful Rebekita. I have been bitten by this spider and its poison is very painful, I had a terrible fever for days." Pashco said, as if giving me a weather report. I sat there frozen to the spot, whimpering quietly, as the Shaman and Pashco continued to eat breakfast as though nothing had happened.

Most of all, I enjoyed walking through the rainforest with the Shaman, and always felt a warm glow of belonging during these times alone with my teacher. We had neither a compass, nor supplies, but we never got lost. Don Juanito had lived in the rainforest for most of his life, and he knew the pulsating rhythms of its heart like his own. We always walked in silence, but my mind was constantly chattering, full of questions about everything, inspired by the richness, fertility and abundance of this ancient forest.

"Don Juanito, do you believe in good and evil?" I asked one day as we were out walking. The Shaman looked at me in surprise. "The whole of nature is hanging between the delicate balance of good and evil. Without the dark, there can be no light, and without the light, there can be no dark."

"But sometimes it is hard to see the light when we are surrounded by so much negativity and darkness."

"Do not despair, Rebekita, because in truth there is no such thing as evil. This is just a judgement for those who have forgotten that the divine light of love exists within them."

"But at the moment the world seems to be dominated by evil people."

I looked on disconcertedly as the Shaman roared with laughter.

"Rebekita," he said, "our lives are filled with the struggle between good and evil, for both live within us. The journey is not outside of us, but an inner journey. It is every person's right to choose the path they wish to take. We can choose to allow the compassionate and loving side of us to grow and flourish, regardless of what is happening around us. Or we can decide to be controlled by negativity and fear. Be very clear, there is no right or wrong path. That is what it means to have free will."

"What do you mean, surely to walk in love and light is better than to walk in fear and darkness?" I protested.

"No, no, no Rebekita, no one can judge another's path. But if you choose to walk the path of fear, you choose a life full of suffering and misery."

"That's easy for you to say, living here safe in the rainforest. It's confusing and scary out there in the real world. Our structures and systems are breaking down, and our leaders are no longer listening to the people." I argued back, annoyed at the Shaman's apparent ignorance as to what was happening in the world.

"Rebekita, the world is only what we create it to be. We have chosen to live in a world controlled by fear, and dominated by force. Do not be mistaken. By accepting this choice, we are all responsible for making the *brujos* very powerful. They are only in power because we allow them to be."

"What is a *brujo*?"

"A *brujo* is one that inflicts illness and disease through force, which can take many forms. The disease and pain caused by *brujos*, both in my country, and in yours, is very real. War, and the bombs and weapons that we fight with, are the physical manifestations of control, hate and fear. Here in the rainforest I have actually extracted thistles that have been magically placed in the victim's body by the *brujo* to make them sick," the Shaman said softly.

"The problem is that the shaman in my country are not very visible, if they exist at all," I replied.

"Ahh, do not doubt. There are many shaman all over the world, spreading their love and light. These are the people who have decided to walk another way, to walk the path of personal responsibility. They are choosing love at every moment, realising that a harmonious life only comes from within. More and more are choosing the way of the shaman, for it is a path that will lead to inner happiness, and ultimate freedom."

"How can we be truly free, when our leaders and politicians seem to be so corrupt, and there is so much injustice in the world. How can we be free when so many people are trapped in a cycle of poverty, perpetuated by governments and business?" I asked.

"It is easy to blame your leaders, but are they not simply a reflection of a greater sickness? Like I have said before, change can only come about when we as individuals decide that we want to change, and live life another way. When we choose the path of love over the path of fear. It is only when enough individuals start living this way that we can create a new world."

"Don Juanito, that's impossible, it would mean changing all our paradigms, our myths, our stories. It would mean creating a whole new reality." I said in disbelief.

"The first step to change starts with you Rebekita, so don't dismiss anything until you can either prove, or disprove it. Believe me, or not, but make your decision with the wisdom of experience," said the Shaman. "There is more to say and I can see from your face that you have many more questions. They will have to wait until later. Now it is time to return. Pascho will have prepared lunch and Don Lucho is coming. He is a friend of ours and will be staying with us for a while."

\* \* \*

A few days later we were all gathered in the kitchen, having a very serious discussion about the lack of yucca. There had been a good harvest but because there had been more mouths to feed than normal, our supply had run low. Don Lucho was an agriculturist who lived on the Rio Blanco. He owned over one hundred thousand hectares of land, which he had cultivated to grow yucca, vegetables and fruit. He had been selling his produce to the surrounding villages, and was planning to return to his farm a six hour walk across the rainforest.

After much discussion it was decided that Pashco, the Shaman, Ramon, Jovino and I would go with Don Lucho to bring yucca back, and stay a couple of days on the Rio Blanco. With this agreed, we hurriedly packed our bedding and some changes of clothing. I was really excited to be able to explore another part of the rainforest, and see Don Lucho's eminent farm, which was famous throughout the region. I was also looking forward to the physical challenge and a change in scenery.

"Rebekita, wear your *botas*. There may be some mud but it should be a relatively easy walk," the Shaman mentioned in passing. I noticed that he was wearing his, but Pashco was walking barefoot. Just before we set off my heart gave out a prayer of gratitude for this adventure.

We left the house and began our walk inland to meet the Rio Blanco further up stream. I was familiar with the first part of the journey, having walked it before. We were heading towards the next village, a competitor in the interregional football tournaments. The selva was very beautiful on the way to the village, full of dense foliage, large lianas, orchids and tall trees. As we approached the village there was a steep hill to climb, a rarity in the rainforest. At the top of the hill lay the local school, and directly in front of it was the football pitch, on the only flat patch of ground. The rest of the village was made up of *casitas* dotted all around the slopes of the hill. It puzzled me that the villagers would build a football pitch on top of a hill but this was the spirit of the rainforest, to find opportunity in the challenge.

We walked down the hillside and stopped at some friends of the Shaman. We had drinks and relaxed, because there would be no other resting place until we reached the Rio Blanco. It also gave Don Juanito and Pashco time to catch up on the local gossip. Soon we were on our way, walking single-file, following a narrow path with dense rainforest on either side of us.

"Watch out Rebekita," called Pashco, as she grabbed my arm. Looking down I saw a thin snake about thirty centimetres long with a blue-green tinge still twitching in front of me, his head lying to one side of the path. It had slithered across the trail, and Ramon had killed it only moments before, with his machete. "This is one of the most dangerous snakes in the rainforest, one bite and a person is dead in two minutes," she told me gravely. It brought me back to my senses. My mind had become so absorbed in itself that I had been oblivious to what was happening around me.

After that I tried to keep my mind focused on the present, to become more aware of the beautiful rainforest we were passing through. We had picked a good day to make the journey, as it was a challenging walk and the sky was cloudy, blocking the harsh rays of the sun. We passed through different parts of the forest, up hills and down valleys, passed streams that flowed into the Rio Blanco, and little *casitas* dotted here and there. I wondered how these people survived so far away from any community or village. Pashco told me that people only needed a clean water supply, which the streams provided. The land itself was fertile and it was relatively easy to cultivate yucca, and other vegetables. I started to think about our cities and towns in the West, bloated with people that had lost all awareness of their connection to the land, filling their lives with empty needs that create mountains of waste, and in the process destroying the purity of that which is so freely and abundantly given to us by nature.

At one point we reached a deep ravine with only the trunk of a tree spanning its width. My heart stopped when I saw it. I had already crossed a number of tree trunk bridges, but none had been as long or as dangerous as this one. I was immediately reminded of my fall down the mountainside, in Machu Picchu, and I felt a wave of fear flow through me. If I fell this time, I would die. No one else seemed to be fazed, and they all just continued walking across the bridge to the other side. It was only my mind that saw it as an obstacle. The Shaman, who was in front of me, went on ahead, but I was frozen to the ground and could not move. The Shaman, realising I was not following, stopped and turned round. "Come Rebekita, do not be afraid. You are safe. You can do it."

"I can't. I can't go forward," I panicked.

"Rebekita, the fear is only in your mind. Do not let your mind stop you from crossing this bridge just because you don't like its form. It still works the same way," the Shaman coaxed.

I put one foot on the trunk, convinced that I would fall, as fear and terror surged through my body. I was nearly in tears. I had to either cross the bridge, or return back to the village alone, and I didn't know what to do. As I stood there, my mind in turmoil, I heard someone come up from behind, and felt Jovino grab my shoulders. "Just stare straight ahead and use your powerful mind to assist you, rather than hinder you, " he whispered into my ear.

"What do you mean?" I asked.

"The only thing stopping you is your fear. You have chosen to believe that the bridge is not safe and that you could fall and die. But this is only a thought. Change this around. Believe that the bridge is safe and secure, and you cannot fall. See it in your mind's eye, and make it your reality. Do not allow this fear of the bridge, that only exists if you allow it, to stop you from completing your journey."

I could see everyone waiting for me patiently on the other side of the ravine, and knew I could not let them down. Having already come so far, it was impossible to turn back now. As Jovino had instructed, I imagined crossing a bridge made of steel, with steep walls that protected me. The fear gradually began to dissolve as I walked across the trunk. By the time I had reached the other side, the limitations of a past experience had been released into the ravine, and I felt empowered and strong.

Once safe on the other side a rush of adrenaline filled my body, and I began to laugh with relief. I felt lighter, although mentally exhausted, and my legs still felt wobbly as we left the forest and started walking through fields of lush grass. Climbing a high hill, views of the surrounding area took my breath away. We rested at the top and ate some fruit that was growing on the trees. The walk had been harder and longer then we had anticipated, and we were all tired. As we neared Don Lucho's farm, an old Eagles song started playing in my head the words reflecting my experience. *"You may lose or you may win but you will never be here again, so lighten up...,"*. On the bridge, I had learnt that it is only fear that stops us completing our journey. When we face the fear and take risks, in order to experience everything life has to offer, we know we cannot lose or win. Instead, we grow and evolve.

We finally arrived late in the afternoon, and it had been worth the challenge. The farmstead was stunning, fertile and abundant. There was total silence, with no other *casitas* for miles. After we prepared our *mosquiteros* on the veranda of the main *casita*, I was shown the general direction of the Rio Blanco. Grabbing my towel I went to wash and cool myself down. The Rio Blanco, despite being a fast flowing river during the rainy season, was now more like a cool, refreshing stream. There was no one around, and so I took the risk of bathing naked, something I hadn't done since being in the rainforest. I always washed in my swimming costume and a sarong, on our busy river.

I will never forget the memory of bathing naked in the river, alone, as the sun was setting over the farm painting the sky the most magical pinks, oranges and reds that vibrated and shimmered. My mind was quiet and I was at peace with myself, too exhausted to think of the dangers that may or may not happen. I had faced a big fear and felt relaxed, happy and content. It was as if this special place was reflecting the harmony and peace within me. Everything was perfect. I sat in the river until the sun had sunk into the horizon, and a glow spread across the sky. Then fatigue hit, and I barely had the strength to walk back to the casita. Collapsing in my mosquito net, I instantly fell asleep, despite the fact that I was lying on the hard wooden slats that made up the floor.

The next morning we awoke late, relaxed, and ate, and ate, and ate. The farm was famous for its produce, and Don Lucho and his wife, Yolanda, were very hospitable. We ate cocona, (a small, round yellow vegetable), pineapple and sugar cane. They killed a chicken, which was prepared with rice. We had fish soup, platano, and fried banana, and we drank endless amounts of sweet masato. That afternoon, Pashco, Don Lucho, Yolanda and I went to find yucca to prepare more masato, and to take back to our village. It was a slow and easy afternoon, reflecting the peacefulness of the farm.

After we had harvested enough yucca, we sat around talking about cultivating the rainforest, and the difficulties of overseeing such a huge amount of land. There was a lot of laughter and joking, as we drank colmena, a mild, naturally produced alcohol, which was delicious. I sat silently, listening to the banter and jokes, seeing the interaction between the families, and was reminded of my own family and friends. People are ultimately the same, all over the world, regardless of the communities, cultures, or religions in which we live. We all love to relate, to laugh, to play, to cry, to share experiences and connect with each other, and despite my Western cultural differences, I found a common meeting point through humour, stories and human interactions.

As darkness fell, Don Lucho and Yolanda went to fish. During the day the sun beats down on the river, making it hot, so fish swim at a deeper level, whereas at night they come closer to the surface. Don Juanito, Pashco, Don Lucho's children Estella and Hernan, and Jovino, were sitting on the porch, and I was teaching them how to play spoons, a fast and fun card game. We all sat in a circle and put five spoons in the middle, because there were six of us. The aim of the game is to make a full suit of clubs, diamonds, spades or hearts by rejecting one card and giving it to the person next to you, and taking the card they have rejected. Once a person has four cards, of the same symbol and number, they grab a spoon. Then, all the other players have to take a spoon, and the one who is too slow, is out of the game. Soon we were shrieking with laughter, as Hernan grabbed a spoon, and we all scrambled and fought for the remaining spoons.

Suddenly, the Shaman, who had lost the last round and was lying down relaxing, sat up sharply and began murmuring under his breath in *Quechua*, his local language. I didn't take much notice of him, as we continued to play. He turned to Pashco, and said something to her. She went into the *casita*, and came out with a bottle of *Agua de Florida*. The Shaman took a swig, spitting it out around us, and around the porch. He did this a number of times. Shocked, we stopped the game, and looked at him. He then blew tobacco smoke over the porch using his pipe, and began cursing that he did not have any other protection with him.

I thought he had gone mad, and asked him what was happening. In a fearful voice, he told me we were being visited by a very dangerous and malicious *brujo*. I looked at him in surprise. Nothing seemed different to me, but I could not deny the change in Don Juanito's energy, and he was certainly acting a little strange. He looked truly nervous. Jovino, Estella and Hernan also picked up the Shaman's energy and looked at me questioningly. Shrugging it off as supernatural nonsense, I decided to ignore the Shaman, and started playing the game again.

Suddenly, Estella gripped me by the arm. Her face had gone white, and there was fear in her eyes. "Rebekita," she said in a frightened whisper, "we are in big danger, please pray for us." Her fear was infectious, and I began to feel scared myself, but did not know why. I looked at the Shaman, who by this time was chanting words over and over again, in *Quechua*, invoking all the healing spirits to come and help us, whilst Pashco was still spitting *Agua de Florida* over the porch.

The Shaman gruffly told me to start praying to my God for protection. I didn't know what to do, having left my religious God behind so many years before. Involuntarily, I started reciting an old Jewish prayer that I used to say every night as a child, but my heart wasn't really in it. I could believe in a lot of things, but dangerous *brujos* was stretching the imagination too far. I was a Westerner, and did not believe in these things.

Everything went deathly silent, and then I heard it, a sound that even to this day, when I think about it or tell this story, sends shivers up my spine. It was a sound from some distance away, in the depths of the forest. I had never heard it before, and never heard it again after that night. It was like a mechanical whirring noise that started low, and got higher, and higher. Goosebumps appeared and the hairs on the back of my neck and arms stood on end. A cold shiver ran down my spine as the sound started to get closer, and I began to tremble as the icy sensation spread throughout my body. I was scared. Very scared. This was no joke. I could sense the danger we were in as I became aware of the dark energy of the *brujo*, and knew it was real. The night seemed to get terribly black as the sound approached us. As it got nearer, Estella burst into tears, and the Shaman chanted loudly and with force, but the fear was in his voice.

I prayed to the universe for our safety and protection, not knowing what else to do. I was being shown the magic and wonder of the *selva*, and given first hand experience of the power of *brujos* and shaman. The sound got close, but not too close, and slowly we heard it recede into the distance, until it reached the far edge of the forest, and was gone. We sat in silence and shock for a while. Slowly, the night seemed to get brighter, and the nocturnal rainforest sounds returned.

The Shaman breathed a sigh of relief, as the energy around us returned to normal, and we all began to laugh, dissipating the fear that had built up among us. I was scared to go to the toilet, but the Shaman assured me that the danger had passed. Walking guardedly down the steps I wandered behind the *casita*. The rainforest no longer felt as safe and secure. Just as in the urban jungle of London, there were unknown dangers and evils lurking around every corner. The difference was that here the rules were clear, *brujos* were evil, shaman were healers and the world seemed to have a natural order. Here was simplicity, a harmony that just did not seem to exist in the chaos of London.

Later that night, a light shining through my mosquitero woke me. I thought it was the Shaman shining his torch, but it was the rising moon. The stars were glistening and gleaming in the cold night sky, and a light mist hovered over the farm. The moon, huge and full, cast her silver light, and I could still feel the magic and wonder in the air. I left the porch and walked someway into the mist, until sure I would not be seen, and removed my clothes. Naked, I let the soft rays of the moon bathe me.

As I absorbed the power and rhythm of the Amazon, I heard a voice in my head say, *"Nature is harmony, and harmony is power, because it does not doubt what it is. You are part of its magic and it is a part of you. Only when you become who you truly are will you find the key to happiness. Now you must believe who you are, trust it, and live it at every moment."*

I did not know what the message meant but I was overcome with bliss as the light of the moon cleansed my body.

# CHAPTER SEVEN

## *Losing My Identity*

A day after our return from the Rio Blanco, I awoke late and lay under my *mosquitero*, anger surging around my body, my head whirling with questions and doubts. I was relieved that the room was deserted, so that no one could be on the receiving end of my raging emotions. Ramon and Jovino had left early, to go hunting, while Elsa and her sister were visiting their mother who lived in the village. There is little privacy in the rainforest. The only space to myself was at night, under the protection of the mosquito net that I tucked into the corners of my mattress, (considered a luxury in the rainforest, as most people sleep on the ground). I was sleeping in the big main room opposite Ramon, Esther, Elsa and the baby. I always wondered how they all slept under the *mosquitero* so peacefully, without ever complaining.

I really missed my family, and wondered if they were missing me. They were so far away, in another life. I was following my dream, but I didn't really belong here in the rainforest. Now I wondered whether I even belonged in London with my family and friends. Things were so unreal, so far from anything familiar, and there was no one to share my experiences with, no one who could really understand me.

One of my major concerns was that we still had not taken Ayahuasca. I felt ready, especially after all the things that had already happened to me. I was learning so much about myself, surely I was now sufficiently prepared to take the sacred brew? Obviously, Don Juanito thought I was still not ready, and a surge of pent up frustration flooded through me, focused at the Shaman.

I breathed deeply, and waited until the emotions had abated before I packed my bed up and wandered into the kitchen. Don Juanito looked up, saying nothing. Pashco, sitting by the fire, nodded. I sensed that she was uncomfortable with my presence there, disrupting her routine, her time with Don Juanito, and her carefully structured life. Their silence made me feel guilty for lying so long in the *mosquitero*, giving me the impression that the Shaman was judging me for this, which only fuelled my anger. I sat down moodily beside Don Juanito, while Pashco expertly re-ignited the dying embers of the fire, heated up the fish soup, and made me some coffee. They had eaten their own breakfast hours before.

"Today, after you have eaten, we will go by canoe down the river. I want to show you a lake that is considered a very special place, with lots of spirits," said the Shaman, surprising me. I had prepared myself for a sarcastic remark about my late appearance, but it had not come.

"Okay, whatever you want to do," I said, grouchily.

"It is also well-known for its fish, and we will need to catch some for tomorrow's lunch, in case Ramon and Jovino are not successful in the hunt. If they are, we will smoke them for when we go to *El Centro* – which will be soon. You have come just at the right time, because soon it will be impossible to enter the lake. We are now in the dry season and the river is receding very quickly," Don Juanito replied cheerfully, ignoring my bad mood.

"So where is the lake?" I asked my curiosity aroused.

"Patience, my little *linda wawita*, you will know in good time. First you must eat and fulfil your physical hunger, and then your mental hunger and only then you will be given the opportunity to fulfil your spiritual hunger." Don Juanito said teasingly. But I was in no mood for his banter. "Why do you call me that?" I asked indignantly.

"Call you what?" said the Shaman innocently.

*"Linda wawita,"* I replied.

"Because children make the sound of *waawaa*, and you are still a little child, *mi hija,*" he replied with a smile.

The Shaman was just provoking my already fragile state and I didn't know how to react. I was trying so hard to fit in, and be mature about everything, even though it was all so different. All he could do was joke. Was he not aware of what I was going through? Suddenly I felt my anger beginning to boil over, and in the anger, found courage to broach the subject of taking Ayahuasca with him.

"Don Juanito?"

"Yes, Rebekita"

"When will we take Ayahuasca?"

"We will take it when you are ready. You are still not prepared enough – *falta tiempo*. There is something you must come to terms with, and until you have overcome this test, the Ayahuasca cannot be taken," the Shaman said, voicing my suspicions.

"But I have been through so much. Will I *ever* be ready?"

The Shaman laughed at the sight of my sad face. "So much impatience Rebekita. When the time is right, you will know and only then will you be truly ready. The teacher appears only when the pupil is properly prepared. Do not hurry the process." I doubted whether there would ever be a time when I was not tested or coming up across some obstacle. I was learning so much about life, but I wondered when the Shaman would actually start teaching me about shamanism. I tried to find out precisely when it would be the right time to take Ayahuasca, but the Shaman did not want to engage in conversation anymore. He seemed content and at peace, looking out across the river, watching the men pass by on their way to fish and find food in the deeper parts of the rainforest, whereas I was getting overwhelmed by all the thoughts and feelings that were tying me up in knots.

Don Juanito stood up and straightened his clothes. "Come Rebekita, get your things together, there is a lot to learn today."

Distracted from my thoughts, I went to the main room to get my machete and spied my money pouch, peeping out the top of my rucksack. I immediately got a very strong feeling to take it with me. It contained all my material possessions, my passport, credit cards, about seven hundred and fifty US dollars, two hundred pounds sterling, my return airline ticket, various addresses and receipts, and Harry's gold signet ring that he gave me at the airport. I usually left the pouch in my rucksack, but my intuition was very strong, and I decided to follow it. I didn't want to leave myself vulnerable, if it was stolen.

Grabbing the money belt, I tied it around my waist, while following the Shaman down to the river's edge, where our canoes were moored. The canoes were made out of a special wood from the rainforest, hollowed out, with wooden slats as seats. Don Juanito owned four canoes of varying sizes, and chose the smallest one. Nimbly, he leapt into the canoe and steadied it, as I gingerly, yet as elegantly as possible, stepped inside. I had still not perfected balance in the smaller, less stable canoes, and as I stepped in, the boat rocked violently and I nearly got thrown over the other side of it. The Shaman laughed in delight at my embarrassment, and I blushed a deep red, wondering if I would ever get anything right. I got myself seated comfortably, the Shaman thrust a paddle in my hand, and we began to row upstream, along the river's edge.

The person in the front of the boat does most of the work, and sitting behind the Shaman gave me the time to look around, and every so often steer the boat in the right direction. The sun was very hot on my face and head, but there was a cool breeze on the river. The rainy season was at an end and the rainforest was a mass of green hues, dancing in the sunlight, whilst the river, dark and deep, contrasted with the blues of the sky. We meandered our way upstream, passing a number of *casitas* dotted along the riverbank where some of the women were washing clothes, or collecting water in big buckets. As we paddled past they waved, shouting greetings and snippets of local news. Everyone knew the Shaman – he was a local celebrity, and one of the oldest men in the area.

The *casitas* petered out as we got deeper into the forest. I attempted another conversation with the Shaman, who wasn't listening, so I got myself comfortable, trying to enjoy the moment. But my mind was restless. My eyes rested on my money belt, and a new train of thought started.

Before I had arrived in the rainforest I had been concerned about money. In fact, I was always concerned about money, and whether I had enough of it. Even though I now had plenty, I still wondered whether it was a sufficient amount to keep me going in the rainforest. I did not know how much learning about shamanism cost, nor how much the Shaman would charge me. He had already discussed with me his thoughts about money, and I did not want to offend him by bringing the concept of money into the training, especially as I had been guided here. I also didn't want to have the issue of payment lurking in the background, and I just didn't know the rainforest etiquette. In order to find peace of mind I had to find a way of bringing up the subject before the training started.

Having made the decision to discuss the issue of money with the Shaman, my mind slowed down, allowing me to become more aware of where I was, and what I was doing, for the first time that day. We were heading for a special lake, renowned for its fish, and it was time to stop worrying and start enjoying myself. I breathed in the cool, fresh air and let it fill my lungs. It tasted sweet and salty, thick with the vitality of the rainforest. Gradually, I became aware of the slap of the paddle hitting the water, and the unique rainforest sounds of the insects and birds.

It is hard to capture in words my feelings of peace, laying in that canoe on the river, on a hot sunny day. The warm breeze ruffled my hair, and the butterflies and dragonflies that hovered overhead sometimes landed to drink the sweat from my skin. The rainforest was captivating, the beauty and fluidity of its colours, shapes and forms were mesmerising, and soon my earlier anger and frustration had melted away. My body relaxed, as all the stress and expectations of taking Ayahuasca no longer seemed that important, and I began to enjoy being in the moment.

Without warning, Don Juanito took a left turn, leaving the river, and followed a smaller tributary towards the lake. This tributary was very shallow and the Shaman informed me that in a month the lake would be cut off, and only accessible by foot. There was evidence of this, as we manoeuvred around fallen tree trunks and big rocks that were usually covered by water. Near to the entrance of the lake, we reached a very low tree trunk that had fallen across the river. It was impossible for us to pass underneath it or to go over it. We paddled the canoe to the riverbank and tied some rope around it. The Shaman pulled from the front, I pushed from behind, and together, we dragged the canoe along the bank until we had passed the tree.

Negotiating the last few bends in the river was difficult. My errors in judging space and depth, as we ducked under trees and avoided boulders, kept the Shaman amused. The tributary was not very wide and the dense forest on either side often joined together, creating a canopy effect that blocked out the sun, and I felt that we were in a green tube of vibrating energy. We took another sharp turn, and there was the lake, laid out in front of us.

It was so beautiful that it took my breath away. The lake was about two kilometres wide, and reflected all the blues of the sky and it's fluffy white clouds. By the river's edge were reflections of the rainforest foliage that surrounded it. Occasionally, a flying fish would leap out of the water landing with a splash a few metres away. Every so often we could hear the monkeys playing and calling each other from the tops of the trees. The place was alive with the sounds of life, echoing around the lake.

There were no other fishermen at the lake. It was as if it belonged to us, a gift for today, and I felt very lucky. Everything was perfect. We paddled into the centre of the lake and the Shaman handed me a fishing rod. "Now we must catch something," he said. I stared at the fishing rod in disbelief. I had never fished before, but I had seen Western rods, and the thing that the Shaman had handed me was something completely different. This was a long thin stick from the rainforest with one thick end and one thin end. At the tip of the thin end was tied a long piece of clear plastic wire with a hook attached to it, and dangling from the hook was a piece of dead fish.

"I've never fished before, and I doubt I will catch anything with this!" I exclaimed.

"Ahh Rebekita, you doubt before you have even tried."

"Well, I didn't mean it quite like that. In the West it is a figure of speech."

"What is a figure of speech?" asked the Shaman.

" Well, I've never really thought about it before, but where I live many people use negative or pessimistic words in their speech without realising it."

"Ah, you are talking about people that speak without awareness of the words that they use."

"Yes, I suppose so. We often use words in every day speech to reinforce an old programme or belief about ourselves, because we do not acknowledge the power and symbolism behind words. Maybe our speech controls our actions more than we realise. I wonder how far speech reflects how we see ourselves and the world around us. Maybe the problem is that we are all too busy speaking unconsciously to actually hear what we are saying".

"This is one of the main hindrances to following our dreams."

"What is?"

"Chattering, gossip, talking unconsciously."

"Why?"

"Most people cannot hear the small voice within them that guides them. The voice of the heart, the higher self, that reminds us of our purpose."

"But can I learn to hear the voice?" I asked.

"Rebekita, only in the silence can you hear this voice. Learn to listen to the voice of your heart, and it will become your key to freedom. In the next few months you will learn to nurture and strengthen the voice inside you until you do not doubt its messages."

We fell into silence, and much to my astonishment, the fish began biting the line. I very soon got into the whole art of fishing. I found it exciting to feel the fish biting, and whipping the line out of the water at just the right angle in order to hook the fish. After a while I got used to the rod, and soon could discern when a fish was just nibbling the line, or if I had a potential catch.

We began to collect a healthy supply of fish for our supper, and I started to ponder on what the Shaman had been saying, and applying it to my own experience. My mind raced back to my time in Machu Picchu, and the silence I had endured there. All the times I had felt isolated with no one to talk to, and had gone running in the mountains, alone. Maybe, if I had listened in the silence, life would have been much easier.

After what seemed like a few minutes, the Shaman broke my reverie. "Okay, the sun is now beginning to set. *Vamos*. We will need to hurry to get back before dark." I looked at the back of the canoe and was amazed at the number of fish that were lying there, to which I had contributed quite effectively. Time had passed so quickly that it hadn't felt as if we'd been there all afternoon. The Shaman must have seen the look of disappointment on my face. "We will come back again for longer, maybe *con cama*." He added. The thought of camping at this wonderful lake filled me with anticipation, and it was something to look forward to. Settling into the canoe, I grabbed my paddle as we made our way back to the little tributary that would lead us to the river.

We followed the flow of the river on the journey home, and this made the controlling of the canoe a logistical nightmare. Paddling upstream had been relatively easy, but on the fast flowing downstream, controlling the canoe was no longer easy. The sun was beginning to set quite rapidly, with branches and rocks appearing out of nowhere as we sped round the bends. Suddenly, looming in front of us was the huge tree trunk, blocking the way. "Turn to the left, to the left" the Shaman shrieked, as we hurtled towards it.

I panicked. Which was my left? It was too late. Instinctively, I stood up to grab onto the trunk, hoping to alleviate some of the force as we slammed into it. As I pushed us away, the canoe rocked violently from side to side, and losing all sense of balance I was thrown over the edge. Coughing and spluttering, I re-emerged to see the Shaman doubled up in hysterics. I swam to the river's edge, and the Shaman steered the canoe to greet me. Sopping wet and laughing, we dragged the canoe past the tree and clambered in. The worst was behind us. I breathed a sigh of relief as I saw the turning to our river ahead of us. The sun had disappeared, and only the orange and pink glow of the sunset illuminated the way. The first stars of the night were already out, twinkling in the deepening blackness.

We turned right, and headed downstream. I stretched out, enjoying the effortless journey as the current took us towards the village. What a perfect day it had been. However, I couldn't relax totally, as something niggled at my peace. Something was wrong, but I didn't know what it could be. A cold vicelike grip clutched my heart and my body went numb, as my brain fought to keep it from my conscious thought. I didn't want anything to spoil this mood. I was feeling so happy, so trusting. Slowly, I glanced down, and the reality hit, sending a rush of panic through my body. The money pouch was no longer tied around my waist.

In despair, I remembered everything I had in it. Everything that connected me to the Western world was in that pouch. It was my identity, and it contained Harry's irreplaceable signet ring! "Stop the boat!" I screamed at the Shaman, almost in tears as the enormity of the situation began to dawn on me. "Don Juanito, I have lost my pouch," I choked out, as he gently pulled the canoe to the side of the riverbank. He looked on unconcerned as I frantically searched the canoe, scrabbling amongst the dying fish, praying that the pouch had fallen off while I had been sitting in it. I must have lost it in the tributary on the way back from the lake, but it was not possible to go back now that night was setting in. This was a nightmare. My worst fear had come true.

I searched every inch of the canoe in a blind panic. Thoughts of having to return to Iquitos, or maybe even Lima, gripped me in fear. "What am I going to do? What the hell am I going to do?" I muttered, over and over again, almost hysterical. "Don Juanito, please help me. What shall I do?" I pleaded, feeling very vulnerable in a situation that was way beyond my control.

*"Dios es Grande,"* he answered, looking me deep in the eyes. I stared at him in disbelief. What the hell did that mean? God is great! At a time like this! Believing and following a dream was one thing, when I had only something as intangible as my faith to lose. This was totally different, now my pouch was lost and I was stuck, miles away from civilisation.

'God is Great... God is Great... *trust your heart,*' kept reverberating around my mind, but I had no idea how this was of any practical use. I was completely fucked.

"Don Juanito, please tell me what to do," I begged.

"Ahh, Rebekita, hear your heart. Only you can decide, but remember, God is Great," he answered.

"But I don't believe in God," I protested.

"Rebekita, when I say God I am meaning the higher part of who you are, your higher self. Not the ego, or the personality, but the all-powerful part of every human being. We do not believe we have everything we need within us, but we are all aspects of the One, and the One is experiencing life through us. Through freedom of choice we are able to experience everything. You've chosen what you want to experience, so be happy."

"Don Juanito, are you saying that we actually choose what happens in our lives, and that God is not the cause of what happens to us, but a part of us?"

"Yes, Rebekita, we are not separate from God, we are all different experiences of God."

"That would mean that we would have the power to create whatever we want to. But if we really could make whatever we want to happen, why would I choose to lose my money belt?" I asked, confused.

" Remember, everything is given to us by ourselves, as a test. Maybe it is the test of attachment, maybe the test of letting go, maybe the test of learning to give and receive. Whatever the reason, every test brings us closer to an understanding of who we truly are. When things happen that we do not like, we fight with life, instead of accepting things as they are. We forget to see the greater picture, and so fail to see the new challenges that each moment gives us, the opportunities that arise when something changes. We must learn to let go of trying to control life, and let our higher selves live us. Life then has a funny way of turning out just right, and we can see the perfection in everything. In your particular case, this experience is an opportunity to see how much passion you have for your dream. Are you ready to throw away your dream for documents, and bits of paper that prove nothing about who you truly are?"

I stared at the Shaman's wise handsome face. His words were comforting, but what did he know of the legalities? He was a man of the rainforest, not of the city where these papers were essential. "Don Juanito, I don't think you understand the implications of this. I have lost my money, my passport with my Peruvian visa in it, my airline ticket, all my documents, everything. What am I going to do?" I demanded, as calmly and rationally as I could.

"What are you saying, that official documents are proof that you exist, and without them, you don't?" the Shaman replied patiently.

"No, not like that," I said, exasperated at his philosophical answer and his apparent lack of concern about my crisis. "I mean that every person needs to be identified in some way, and these documents prove that we are who we say we are."

"But whose identity are you following, Rebekita? Is your identity connected to your heart or to your society? Listen to your heart – only your heart has the answers."

Suddenly it dawned on me that the woman represented by the passport, the money, and the documents didn't really exist. At that moment the only thing that existed was Rebekita, in a blind panic, sitting in a canoe full of dead fish on a river at sunset. My heartbeat slowed, as I began to comprehend more fully the lesson I needed to learn, and the challenge I needed to overcome. Breathing deeply I tried to think rationally again, and knew I had only two choices. I could stay in the rainforest with no form of identity and no money, or return to Iquitos to sort it out. Somehow, I knew that if I left the rainforest I would not come back. Here, now, in this moment, I had the opportunity to learn about shamanism and healing, and become an *Ayahuasquero* like my teacher.

As we made our way back to the *casita*, my mind was in chaos. Suddenly, everything looked very different. I had wasted too much time obsessing about money, and worrying about so many things, when really, they had all been meaningless. My greatest fear had now come true, and I was confronted with my biggest test yet of trust and faith.

The next morning, after a very sleepless night, I knew what I had to do. I had to take the biggest risk of my life, stay in the rainforest, and learn the ways of the Shaman. Not as an identity, nor a number, nor a title, but as a human being, with all my flaws, my rough edges, and my sufferings. I had to let go of the identity created for me by society, in order to find out who I really was.

Intellectually, the decision was easy to make, but it was difficult putting it into practice. For the first few days I awoke feeling physically sick about the whole episode. I spent most of those days berating myself for being stupid enough to lose the pouch. I wasted hours, envisioning that someone would find it so that I would no longer have to fear the consequences. Soon I realised that this was a fruitless endeavour. I just had to accept that the pouch was gone. I began to recognise that my mind was most peaceful when focusing on the present, because then I cared less that I had lost my money, my documents, and Harry's precious ring.

Some days later the Shaman announced that we would take a trip to the *casitas* in the centre of the rainforest, where I would be initiated into Ayahuasca. It was a timely announcement, because just that morning I had woken up for the first time without fear punching my stomach. I was realising that it isn't life that is stressful; it is we who create stress. When we fight life we are actually only fighting ourselves, trying to control things so that they fulfil our needs and desires. It was time to start accepting that the only thing I had any control over were my choices.

After about three hours we were ready to leave. Pascho, Don Juanito, Ramon, Elsa, Esther, the baby and I, our beds and clothes, machetes and some kitchen utensils were all piled into the biggest canoe. At last, we were on our way, with Walter and Lydia waving to us and wishing us good luck. The Shaman, Ramon, Pashco and I started to paddle, and very soon we had found our rhythm, as we headed to another part of the rainforest.

# LOSING MY IDENTITY

* * *

The Shaman and I spent most of our first morning in *El Centro* exploring the pristine rainforest surrounding the *casitas*. It was more dense and wild here, and we left while the sun was still low in the sky with the promise of another hot day. It was cool under the shade of the huge trees that towered above us, and the canopy trapped the luscious smell of the dew, as it dried on the rich green foliage. Leaves crunched under our feet, as we left the trail and plunged deep into the forest. Here, the trees were much closer together, and narrow chinks of light pierced through the gaps in the treetops, illuminating the dark spaces beneath. Unusual and indigenous orchids grew on the trunks, breaking the green monotony with their deep reds and pinks.

After a while, I mentioned to the Shaman that I was thirsty. As we passed some cones lying on the ground the Shaman stopped. Stooping down he picked one up and broke through the shell with his machete, drinking the liquid inside. Tossing it away he picked another one up, and passed it to me. The liquid was sweet and cool and we spent the next hour satiating our thirst with rainforest juice.

As the sun got higher the rainforest seemed to grow quiet and still. Most of the time I was unaware of the subtle movements and activity going on at a physical level. My eyes were unaccustomed to this environment, and could not distinguish between the different shapes in the green gloom. Often Don Juanito would stop to point out the monkeys playing above us, or wild pig tracks, toucans, indigenous flowers, lianas, and medicinal plants that I had not noticed.

While we walked in silence I was struck with a thought that seemed to come from this ancient *selva*, the lungs of this planet. It told me that the rainforest is like a mystical prophet that transmits its messages in the silence, and the shaman, its disciple, digests its teachings. I was as yet unable to hear the wisdom of this place, and in time hoped that I too would learn to hear its messages. All I needed to do was surrender to the Shaman, my teacher, just as he surrendered to the Amazon. Already there were moments when I felt connected to the animals, the Shaman, nature, and myself, when I no longer felt separated from the life force that binds us together, and in these moments I was truly happy.

We returned later in the day, and after a fulfilling lunch of fish soup, yucca and rice, I lay in my hammock under the shade of two trees, staring up at the clouds trying to discern faces and patterns in them. Don Juanito was lying in one of the *casitas*, dozing, little snores escaping from his open mouth. Ramon had gone fishing for food, and Pashco had gone to the stream to bathe with Elsa and Esther. It was quiet, peaceful and isolated here in *El Centro*, compared to the chaos of the other home on the river, with Lydia, Walter and the children always around, and a constant stream of visitors from the village.

Abruptly, Walter and Lydia came bursting into the middle of the clearing, out of breath and very excited, disturbing the peaceful calm of the afternoon. I was surprised to see them, as they had not planned to join us. Something important must have happened for them to paddle all the way from the village, just to give us a message. It was a tiring canoe trip and a long walk to reach the *casitas*.

Walter started shouting at Don Juanito to wake up, and Pashco came running from the stream to see what all the commotion was about. "They've found your pouch," I heard Walter gasp, flushed and red as he approached us. "A local fisherman was near the lake and hooked your pouch. Everyone is talking about it, but come, you must come back to the village now, and identify it. No one has seen it with their own eyes, but the rumour is that nothing has been damaged by the water, and that all the money is there."

As Pashco, Elsa and Esther began to organise my passage back to the village to reclaim my pouch, all I could do was just stand there, in the clearing of the rainforest, as the reality hit me. Had I consciously created the finding of my pouch? I did not know for sure, but it certainly was my greatest dream come true. I turned to the Shaman to thank him, but he just smiled his knowing smile. "Sometimes, Rebekita, we just have to let go, and believe that we are creating everything, at every moment. You are learning that we cannot judge if something is right or wrong, good or bad, negative or positive. When we trust that we are doing the right thing and following our hearts, we know that everything is happening perfectly. But more importantly, your faith is strong, and you are starting to find out who you truly are. You are now ready to take your first journey with Ayahuasca."

# CHAPTER EIGHT

## *Preparation for Ayahuasca*

Two days after my pouch had been found, I returned to *El Centro* with the Shaman, Pascho, and Jovino, who had recently arrived from Iquitos. The money had been wrapped in plastic for protection but it was still a miracle that everything in the pouch was undamaged, apart from my passport photo that had disintegrated. The fisherman had taken some dollars, and I had to pay the locals for retrieving it, but there was still some left. As the news spread around the village and surrounding area, I became known as the *'gringa loca'*.

I was very excited at the thought of taking Ayahuasca at last, but once we had arrived at *El Centro* we continued to cultivate the *chakras* and plant watermelon, yucca and maize. Don Juanito told me that this would make my body, hands and arms strong, and that a shaman needs to be physically fit and healthy. Initially, I felt frustrated by this. I had been tested, had passed the tests with flying colours, and now, despite being mentally ready, the Shaman said I had to be physically fit as well. I was starting to think that the obstacles to taking this plant would never end. But things had changed, because I trusted that the Shaman knew best.

Working in the *chakras* in *El Centro* was different from working in those by the river. There, my mind had been filled with worries of the unknown things that were yet to happen, and concerns for the people who loved me in England. Here, away from everything, my mind was much calmer and quieter. In many spiritual traditions physical work is considered to be an important part of the apprentice's training, and now I understood why. Turning my mind inward, concentrating on the various tasks, and being much more aware of the present moment, I found that sowing and planting were becoming a silent meditation, and an opportunity to integrate some of what I was learning. I was also developing a deep respect for my body.

The next morning we planted maize early, hoping to beat the heat of the sun, for I had been warned it was hard work. First, I made a hole in the ground about two feet deep, by pounding a pole into the soil, and then Pashco put a handful of seeds into the hole and filled it with earth. I found the work really tough, but I couldn't allow Pashco to see me tire, as her stamina never failed to amaze me. Despite her age she was agile and strong, and worked tirelessly, three hundred and sixty five days a year, cooking, cleaning, washing, collecting firewood and water, planting and harvesting, the list was endless. She told me that she had never left Iquitos, never seen snow, or mountains, or the ocean, or sand, or valleys. She had never taken a holiday, and yet I hadn't heard her complain. She accepted her life, and still found the time to laugh and joke.

After about four hours the field was completed. It was only mid morning, but I ached all over, having discovered muscles I rarely used. My face stung with sweat as the heat of the sun glared down on us, and I felt physically sick. We staggered to the *casita*, and I poured a bucket of water over my head. Pashco gave me some *masato* that cooled down my insides, refreshing and revitalising me. Despite my hands being red raw and full of blisters, I felt physically fit and strong, energised in some unexplainable way.

Lying in the hammock, taking a well deserved rest, I took a long, deep, contented breath. The Shaman was lying stretched out next to me on the floor listening to *Shakira* on the portable cassette player. Pashco was in the other *casita*, preparing fish soup for lunch, and the countless green hues that hung over us shimmered in the heat. A flock of parrots flew overhead, screeching and cawing, their colours breaking up the monotony of the deep blue sky. I felt a huge wave of peace and tranquillity swell within me and became filled by the sensation that flowed through my body. Nothing mattered much anymore. Everything was happening perfectly.

I didn't want to be anywhere else, or doing anything else, but lying next to the Shaman, listening to the song *Estoy Aqui* in the shady protection of the *casita*. I turned to him with a beaming smile on my face. He smiled back, and then looking closer, sat up, his pipe dangling from his mouth. We stared silently into each other's eyes. After what seemed like an eternity, he nodded, and muttered something to himself in *Quechua* that I didn't understand. Before I had the chance to ask him, Pashco called us for lunch.

During the meal of boiled yucca, plantain and fish soup the Shaman was in a jovial mood, laughing and teasing Pashco. After eating, they slipped away into the rainforest to be alone. Jovino and I spent the rest of the afternoon chatting and discussing what had been happening to me, and my adventures with the Shaman. I always enjoyed Jovino's company. He was a schoolteacher; the most educated among the Shaman's family, and the one who understood me the most. But I rarely saw him, and his agreement to join me here at *El Centro* for my first Ayahuasca ceremony made me feel special, and somehow safer. Late in the afternoon, the Shaman and Pashco returned. "Come Rebekita, there is something we need to do before sunset," the Shaman said, interrupting us.

In the coolness of the dying sun we set off into the rainforest. The Shaman knew exactly where he was going, and I followed in silence, breathing in the deep healing freshness of the trees and foliage. We came to a clearing, and getting down on his hands and knees the Shaman started scurrying around until he found what he was looking for. A liana – a vine-like branch – was growing under the foliage. Lifting it up he chopped it and looked at the inside. The pattern was like that of a four-leaf clover. Taking his finger he wiped it over the pattern and then licked it. "This is Ayahuasca," he said turning to me. "I have planted a number of vines around this part of the rainforest. No one knows where they are, except me and Pashco. We will need all day to prepare it, and under the new moon, tomorrow night, we will have our first ceremony. You are ready to see whether Ayahuasca will accept you as her pupil."

I felt a shudder of anticipation race down my spine. The waiting was finally over. Suddenly, I realised just how many expectations I had, as my mind became preoccupied with thoughts and fears. To stem their flow I put my mind to the task at hand, trying to remain in the present.

We spent the next hour cutting up the Ayahuasca vine into pieces about twenty centimetres long, and putting them into a sack. There were three types of Ayahuasca to be found in our part of the rainforest, *Cielo Ayahuasca* and *Treno Ayahuasca*, which are medicinal, and *Negro Ayahuasca*, a poison that is only used for hunting animals. After we had filled the sack, we went looking for the plant that is prepared with the Ayahuasca to help induce the visions. After searching around close to where the vine was growing, the Shaman found the plant he was looking for and cut some leaves off. I enquired about them and he told me that *Tauway Hojas* and *Ayuma Corteza* are two hallucinogenic leaves that induce the Ayahuasca visions. We were collecting *Ayuma Corteza*. The Shaman shoved them into the sack as well, and then, sitting under the shade of a tree, he got out his pipe and chanted his songs, thanking the spirits of the forest and the Ayahuasca.

I sat beside the Shaman in the middle of the rainforest, letting the words of the incantations wash over me, while my mind filled up with questions. When the Shaman had completed his chanting and was sitting in a peaceful silence, I asked my question.

"Don Juanito, what exactly is Ayahuasca?"

"Ahh, Ayahuasca. She is the *Mother of all Medicine*. A tool to help you find yourself, to know yourself, by destroying the image of who you think you are, and illuminating the truth. The knowledge that you can acquire from Ayahuasca is not imparted from the great cosmic serpent, or from a source outside of yourself. This is an inner journey, where only love and faith can guide you."

"But how can a medicinal plant help me find myself?"

"Through the visions. She cuts through the veil of illusion and opens your heart."

"That sounds scary," I said.

"It takes discipline, and a strong and courageous person to accept who they are. Many people do not have the courage to see themselves, because they have unconsciously accepted the images and stereotypes created by society. They have forgotten to honour their unique potential, and particular strengths and weaknesses, fearing that deep part of themselves that we keep hidden from each other. With Ayahuasca your true self is illuminated. The dark and light live together in the heart. If you can accept the dark, as well as the light, that is dwelling within you, you can live the Shaman's way."

"What is the Shaman's way?" I asked, intrigued.

"A shaman is someone who walks the path of the heart. A shaman understands their true nature, and lives it by consciously creating his or her reality. My little *linda wawita*, soon you will be master of your heart, and your mind will again become the servant. This will take time, and all apprentices must go through fire to understand the language of the heart. But that is in the future. For now, trust in Ayahuasca without doubt and She will help you."

The Shaman remained silent for a while. I had learnt not to interrupt him, and after some minutes he nodded his head and turned to me.

"Ayahuasca, if She decides to, can show you many things. She will open up the secret doors and remove the veils of illusion to show you truth. But be aware. Once you have opened these doors, there is no turning back. You must be prepared to complete the training, for there are no immediate realisations. It is a journey that you have promised to undertake, and I have agreed to teach to you. Our life's promise is about to be played out. I am the teacher, and you are my apprentice, and there are some rules that you must abide by. Do not question my judgement. Follow the strict diet that Pashco will prepare for you, and trust that this is your destiny. You will learn to heal using Ayahuasca, and you will be initiated into the *Ayahuasquero* tradition. This is sacred knowledge. Use it wisely and with respect. For only then will you receive and be able to access its full power."

Sitting beside the Shaman I heard the enormity of his words. We had both agreed to undertake this journey together. Despite the inherent dangers, I knew I was safe and secure, protected by the Shaman. I could not control what was going to happen tomorrow night. All I could do was take the visionary vine, and trust. If She didn't accept me, then it meant I was still not ready to be initiated. With that thought I felt an immense weight lift from my shoulders, as I became free of the expectations that I had placed on myself.

* * *

The Shaman woke me early the next morning while it was still dark. "Come Rebekita, we have a lot to do today." Bleary-eyed I staggered to the stream and washed my face in the cool water.

When I returned to the kitchen *casita* the Shaman was already there, having begun the preparations. On a flat section of wood, about a foot across, the Shaman was hitting the pieces of Ayahuasca one by one with a wooden baton, banging each piece three times, to splinter and flatten it. It looked like hard work, and I could see the Shaman's arm muscles tensing as the baton hit the Ayahuasca. However, he did not seem to tire. I watched him, as he methodically banged and flattened the vine.

After half the sack was done he got up and handed me the baton. Sitting where the Shaman had been, I tentatively took a piece of Ayahuasca out of the bag and hit it. Nothing happened. The Shaman looked at me with a twinkle in his eye. "No Rebekita. Hit it with strength." Again I raised my arm and bought it down with a loud thud as it made contact with the Ayahuasca. I had splintered it only slightly. It took three or four whacks with the baton before the piece was sufficiently flattened. The second piece took even longer, and already my arm ached. There was no way I was physically going to be able to finish the sack without doing some damage to my limb. I looked up at the Shaman beseechingly. The Shaman looked at me and smiled. "Rebekita, you are concentrating on just hitting the Ayahuasca, which is why it is taking you so much strength to flatten one piece."

"Isn't that what I need to do?"

"Yes, but to make it easier you need to visualise flattening it."

"What do you mean?"

"Do you remember what happened on the log bridge on the way to the Don Lucho's farm? You visualised a safe crossing. Use the same skill here, and imagine flattening the Ayahuasca in two hits. You will find this skill of visualisation useful in every thing you do."

I took another piece out of the sack, and envisioned it being flattened by the first hit. Sure enough the piece of Ayahuasca splintered as if it were a sapling. The Shaman watched me until he was satisfied I was preparing it properly and then left to attend to the next step of the preparation.

By the time the sun had begun to lift itself into the sky we had completed the first stage. In front of me lay a mountain of flattened Ayahuasca, and a number of bruised and battered fingers. My arms ached, and I was dirty and sweaty, but surprised that I did not feel as tired as I had expected.

The Shaman filled his pipe with special rainforest tobacco that has healing properties, and invokes dizziness in the smoker. He lit the tobacco, but instead of inhaling the smoke, he placed his mouth over the roof of the pipe, blowing smoke around a huge cauldron that was only used for preparing Ayahuasca. After the cauldron was filled with smoke he chanted some incantations while putting the splintered Ayahuasca pieces into the huge bowl. He then asked me to fetch enough water from the stream to cover the Ayahuasca and I had to make a few journeys with the buckets. Once the Ayahuasca was completely covered the Shaman added the visionary leaves and tobacco. Finally, he sprayed saliva into the bowl and chanted some more over the completed concoction. We then carefully placed the cauldron onto the roaring fire, and let it cook.

Sitting back down the Shaman looked at me. "Your job today, Rebekita, is to manage the fire. The Ayahuasca needs to cook for most of the day, to ensure the strength of the brew, and that is the reason we got up so early. This is the most important part of the preparation. The fire must never go out, and you mustn't leave the Ayahuasca alone at any moment. *Brujos* can come and tamper with it, and evil spirits can alter the potency and the power of it. It must be constantly protected."

While we sat watching the fire Pashco prepared us breakfast, and I ate hungrily. The Shaman watched me eat. "Rebekita, slow down. Rest while you eat. The hard work has not even started yet." I nodded, my mouth full of food; after hitting all those pieces of Ayahuasca, how hard could tending a fire be?

After breakfast, Jovino went fishing, Pashco and the Shaman went off in search of more firewood, and I was left alone to tend the fire. Already the sun was beating down on the *casita*, where the cauldron was bubbling gently. During the first hour, stoking the fire and tending to the Ayahuasca, I felt genuinely happy and content, excited about taking this *Mother of all Medicines*, and being in ceremony for the first time.

Soon, the sun and the fire turned the *casita* into a sauna, making me drowsy and reflective. Sitting there in the heat I began to drift into reverie, thinking again about my family, my friends, my future, the ceremony that evening, until I was lost in memories and expectations.

"Rebekita, the fire." I heard the Shaman's voice cut into my thoughts. I immediately opened my eyes, saw that the fire was losing its strength and that more wood needed to be added. I looked up at the Shaman, as he and Pashco staggered into the *casita* with bundles of firewood on their backs.

"Rebekita. Wake up! This is not a job for lazy people. You must not fail this very important task. You have to be alert and aware at every moment. If you cannot do this I need to look after the Ayahuasca myself. This is very serious preparation for your own protection," he berated me.

"I am so sorry," I said guiltily. I had fallen so deep into thought I had almost forgotten where I was. "I promise that I will be aware and present until the Ayahuasca is prepared," I answered.

"Good," said the Shaman. "There is enough firewood to last most of the day. Pashco and I will be in the *chakra* and we will return later to have some lunch. But not too much, as the food you take affects the Ayahuasca journey and the benefits of the medicine. Remember, protect the Ayahuasca, and she will protect you".

The Shaman left, and I sat staring at the flames leaping up and around the cauldron. I had promised the Shaman that I would be alert and aware. As I occasionally stirred the Ayahuasca and fed the flames, I tried to concentrate on these actions and not allow my thoughts to wander. Despite my promise, I still found it difficult to stay focused on the present, as my rational mind began to question; what was a Westerner doing, miles away from home, protecting a vine that induces visions from witches that can affect its potency and power?

Soon doubts about myself overwhelmed me, as the Shaman's words reverberated around my head. *You must not fail this very important task*. If the Shaman believed I could fail, how could I believe in myself? Didn't my history prove that I was a failure? Before I could regain control of my mind, the familiar sensation of disappointment started in the pit of my stomach and began to flow around my body, as a deluge of memories from all the times I had failed in my life came flooding back.

Even though I had done so much work on letting go of the past, sitting with the Ayahuasca had once again brought to the surface the same old deep-rooted emotions, beliefs and conditionings that had controlled me for most of my life. I began to feel very sorry for myself, as thoughts flowed like a river after the monsoon rains. Overwhelmed with memories, I started to cry at all the suffering I had experienced during my life, and my feelings of helplessness to stop it.

Then an interesting thing happened. I remembered what the Shaman had taught me. We have chosen everything that has happened in our lives in order to realise who we are. I no longer needed to be a victim of these thoughts. Gradually I started to work out what I needed to learn from this. I was choosing to remain a victim by allowing myself to be controlled by these old experiences.

Letting go of the emotional charge of the thoughts, it became clear that I was still holding on to the need for approval. Then it hit me that what I had been really seeking was my mother's approval. A sleeping volcano deep within me was beginning to stir. This need for approval, and the fear of doing something wrong, of failing, was what had been holding me back for so long.

Instantly, I was again Rebekita, a grown woman, stirring the Ayahuasca cauldron in a swelteringly hot hut in the middle of the rainforest, preparing for initiation into the shamanic tradition of the Peruvian Amazon. I no longer needed to choose to be stuck in the past, and Ayahuasca was the key to help me let go of all those conditionings so that I could really start living in the present.

Stirring the big cauldron, I realised that it was also about accepting change. Life changes, people change, situations change, everything is changing at every moment. Nothing stays the same. Like the flames of the fire that constantly leap and shift forms and patterns, life does the same. And yet the human condition is to hold on to what has come before, constantly reacting according to a preconditioned set of emotions, instead of responding to the moment in a much truer state of awareness.

By the time the Shaman and Pashco returned to the *casita*, I was exhausted physically, mentally, and spiritually. Taking one look at me, the Shaman grinned from ear to ear. He knew that during my time with Ayahuasca I had been through a huge awakening. Ayahuasca had already accepted me as her pupil. The initiation had begun.

"Go, wash and cool down my little *wawita*, Pashco and I will finish off the rest of the preparations. You have done well and protected the Ayahuasca. We will take it after sundown tonight," said the Shaman. I left the *casita* as the sun began its slow descent into the west. Everything seemed sharper and clearer, more in focus. Slowly I made my way to the stream and dipped my burning body into its soothing waters. I poured a bucket of water over my head, letting it numb my mind and wash away the heat. I sat for ages, naked and alone, as the little fish swam past, listening to the sounds of the monkeys playing high above me, and the birds twittering to each other as they prepared for the long night ahead.

After washing my hair and body I began to feel more real, and thought about what had happened in the *casita*. I was an evolved rational human, yet controlled by totally irrational thought processes that were created years ago. And maybe it would be the totally magical world of the rainforest that could bring me back to my senses, and help me let go of conditioning that no longer served me. It was time to face my truth.

The notion that being in the 'wild' rainforest was showing me a more useful way of living than the 'civilised' West made me snigger, which turned into a giggle and soon became a full belly laugh, until tears flowed down my face as I released a store of pent-up energy. I couldn't put any aspect of what was happening to me into a logical framework. I didn't even know if I understood it. But it didn't matter. Tonight I was going to take Ayahuasca.

Calmer, refreshed and rejuvenated, I put on some clean clothes – baggy comfortable trousers and a loose white long sleeved t-shirt that I had saved especially for the ceremony – and made my way to the *casitas*. Even though I was really hungry, the Shaman had only allowed me to eat a little soup and yucca. I had already been on a special diet for a few days, which included food with no salt and spices, and *chichuwacha* (the bark of a tree that is soaked in *traigo*, the alcohol of the rainforest, and used as a preventative, or a cure, for ailments). Although I did not know it at the time, it was to prepare me for taking Ayahuasca.

As the sun dipped behind the trees we removed the Ayahuasca from the fire and decanted the deep reddish-brown liquid into a plastic bottle, through a funnel. It was now ready for drinking. The discarded Ayahuasca shards were buried in the ground and the cauldron was cleaned, ready for the next batch.

I lay in the hammock, relaxing with my eyes closed, trying to remain in the moment. I was aware of the cool breeze brushing against my skin, and let my muscles really untangle themselves. The rainforest was very quiet, and there was a stillness in the air that seemed to be filled with anticipation, as though the rainforest knew that I would be taking Ayahuasca tonight.

"Rebekita, are you sleeping?" The Shaman said softly.

"No, I'm just relaxing." I answered.

"Good, open your eyes. We talked a little yesterday about Ayahuasca. Today I want to tell you more about the *Mother of all Medicine*. She is the most potent and powerful medicine on the planet."

Opening my eyes I sat up, and the Shaman sat down beside me. Together we started to swing on the hammock as the Shaman talked.

"Shaman have been taking Ayahuasca for millennia, the knowledge passing down from teacher to apprentice, to ensure that this valuable wisdom is not lost. This wisdom cannot be taught, only experienced by one who is courageous enough to undertake the journey.

"Ayahuasca is alive. She is a living organism that has the ability to understand and communicate with every animate object in the natural world. Ayahuasca is the bridge that connects humans, animals, and the natural kingdoms around us. A skilled shaman who walks across this bridge can interpret the language of plants and animals and is often symbolised in the Ayahuasca visions as serpents entwined around each other."

"DNA is symbolised as the double helix. Could DNA be the material that constructs the bridge?" I asked, remembering what James Narby had said in his book.

The Shaman looked at me blankly, and went on. "We do not know how the Ayahuasca helps us to understand the healing properties of the plants and foliage that are found in the *selva*. But she does more than just this. Another important gift she gives is to remove the veils to other dimensions that exist parallel to this one. Shaman can physically see spirits during the ceremony and are able to communicate with them. Spirits sometimes help during the healing."

"But how can we see other dimensions? That's impossible. I mean no one has really proved they actually exist," I blurted out. The Shaman looked at me patiently.

"Your scientists and anthropologists will never understand the way this world works, because they do not have the courage to experience it. They read their books and write their theories but they do not know truth. They are arrogant and distracted, listening to their rational minds, trying to make the environment fit into their hypotheses. We are unable to experience other dimensions with our ordinary senses, because they are vibrating at a higher frequency than this dimension. However, we are still all interconnected, and our actions affect them, only not as powerfully as our actions affect the other kingdoms in our world."

"I don't understand what you mean?" I said, confused.

"We are all responsible for each other, for the plant and animal kingdoms and the environment within which we live. If we destroy nature, we are destroying ourselves. The only way to protect the environment that feeds us is by living in harmony with Mother Earth. Instead, we have created a world that only focuses on what it sees and not what it feels. We have allowed the science of the mind to become more meaningful than the wisdom of the heart, becoming so preoccupied with the external world that we have forgotten to look within ourselves. The individual spirit has been ignored.

"We are now almost totally controlled by fear, and therefore believe that we need to control the natural flow of life, the very thing that creates and preserves human existence. This fear could eventually lead to the end of the human race as we know it."

"But how can we die out when we are the most powerful species on the planet?" I protested.

"Huh!" the Shaman snorted. "Mother Nature is alive, and is growing just like humans. Do not think the strange weather patterns, and natural disasters you will start to see across this planet are solely because of global warming. No, it is Mother Earth preparing herself for a new cycle, a new rebirth. Now the time has come for the next phase to take place, and it will be painful for those that do not choose to change. Do not despair my little *linda wawita*. We can still change the direction we are going, but only when we decide to change the way we see the world. Only when we unite, and choose *love* instead of fear, *unity* instead of separation, *power* instead of force, can we stop the destruction that is about to take place. For soon it will be time for Mother Nature to take charge once again. She has been patiently waiting for us to wake up, but she cannot wait much longer. This is what Ayahuasca has told us."

"You mean Ayahuasca has told you all this. But why?"

"Because it is time. There will still be pockets of indigenous people living within the beat and rhythm of Mother Earth's heart, continuing to live and prosper, as there have always been. Shamanic knowledge has kept humans alive for thousands of years, and will continue to do so as we learn to play the game in a different way."

"How?" I asked

"When we live a life full of love, harmony and peace. Our thoughts and ideas have created everything that exists on this earth, nothing else, and it is our attachment to these myths and concepts that keep us locked into selfishness and greed. Now it is time for the balance to be restored."

The Shaman fell into silence, and we sat there swinging on the hammock, both lost in thought. I didn't have anything more to say. I had believed for a long time that we had the potential to head towards destruction, and now the Shaman had confirmed this.

The Shaman suddenly broke the silence. "You are my last pupil Rebekita, and my final attempt at guiding an apprentice to spread this knowledge for the next generation. I am now old, and soon I will die. I have tried to teach Jovino, my son, Walter, my son-in-law, and Pepe, but they have been unable to complete the training. There are only a few authentic shaman left on the planet that have the wisdom to teach and guide an apprentice. Many shaman have become tourist attractions, or allowed themselves to be caught in the web of money and ego. The ancient shaman that walked this path were interpreters who could manipulate the universal energy - form, time and travel - between the different veils that separate our world from the spirit and animal worlds. But in every generation this power has been diluted. Not many apprentices complete the training, as we become weaker and weaker. We are now almost spiritually impotent. But there is still time for a new awakening. The power is still accessible. It just takes courage and discipline."

"Don Juanito, I am not extraordinary or gifted with psychic or special powers. I am just a normal, confused human being, one of six billion on the planet, and a Westerner. Why have you chosen me as your apprentice?" I asked.

"Rebekita, trust that it was our true selves, our higher selves that chose each other. I *am* surprised you are a Westerner. However, I trust that everything is happening perfectly, and that you are aware enough to learn the secrets of the spirit, plant and animal kingdoms and the ancient traditional knowledge of the Amazon. I have read your purpose, and the intention in your heart, and I know it is our destiny. That is all I can say at this time. But you should know that I have never met a Westerner who has even wanted to undertake the training. Most of the white people that come to take Ayahuasca with me are too full of fear and doubt, stuck in a rational way of life that makes this training too difficult. They are so attached to the material world that they take the easy option and try to change the outside; a new job, a new lover, a new house, a bigger car, an exotic holiday, or another drug, but the happiness does not last, because real happiness comes from within," the Shaman replied.

"But I know many Westerners who are trying to help themselves through the power of meditation, visualisation, positive thoughts, affirmations and other techniques. There are many of us who are trying to make a change in our lives," I argued.

"Yes, but these tools can only work when there is absolute faith and a commitment to change, and many people use them without this, being too afraid of change, of going within. There is not much time left, which is why I needed to start breaking down your barriers, in order for you to be able to immediately receive the gifts that Ayahuasca can give you," the Shaman replied.

"Now I understand why it took so long to get to this moment. I was so sure I was prepared, but looking back I can see that I am only really ready tonight," I said, my questions almost answered.

"Yes. Tonight we start the journey with Ayahuasca. You are my first Western pupil, and my last apprentice. I have faith in you. Let us begin."

## PART THREE – REUNION

*All my life I have lived on the*
*Lip of insanity*
*Knocking on doors, wanting to*
*Know answers.*
*The door opens*
*I have been knocking*
*From the inside*

Jalal al-Din Rumi

## CHAPTER NINE

## *Ceremonies and Visions*

Dusk was fast descending, and soon I was going to take my first journey with Ayahuasca. The Shaman was in the main *casita* preparing for the ceremony, and I was alone, lying in the hammock in the smaller *casita*. It was as if I had waited all my life for this moment. I breathed in the sweet rainforest air. I was alive with anticipation. Looking up at the blanket of dark sky spreading from the east, and the first few stars shimmering in the dying sunlight, I noticed the sliver of a new moon hanging by a thread, heralding a new beginning.

A swarm of colourful parrots shrieked as they flew over the *casitas*, and the rainforest sounds became more prominent as the nocturnal animals began to stir. Staring up at the moon, I breathed a big sigh as thoughts tumbled round my head: Would I receive visions? Would I be able to fulfil my promise? Would I die? Would I be reborn?

"Rebekita, it is time, we are ready," the Shaman called to me.

With a serious heart I turned to see the Shaman looking at me from the main *casita*. His pipe was dangling from his mouth, and a faint smile played on his lips.

"Come, do not be afraid," he said.

I turned again to the moon that controls the powerful rhythmic flows of nature, to the stars, and to Mother Earth. "Protect me, look after me, and help me to grow. May I find what I am looking for," I whispered.

I clambered up the ladder and entered the larger *casita*. In the corner sat the Shaman, bathed in a glow of orange kerosene light. For my first ceremony it was just the Shaman and his apprentice. Sitting beside the Shaman I noticed two potions, and other items laid out in front of him, as well as the freshly prepared Ayahuasca brew. Patiently, the Shaman went through the different potions that were used for the ceremony.

There are two powerful medicines that are taken with the Ayahuasca, *El Camphor*, which is camphor cubes soaked in *traigo*, and *Agua de Florida*, which is perfumed water. The Shaman drinks these potions during the ceremony to assist him in the healing of the patients and to enhance the visions. Sometimes the Shaman will use *Pomada Una de Gato*, a waxy substance used for massaging rheumatism, arthritis and muscular disorders. There was also the Shaman's pipe filled with rainforest tobacco. The tobacco is used as a healing tool that is smoked and blown around the patient's head and body to clear the energy.

Lastly, one of the most important instruments of the ceremony is the *shacapa*. This is a cluster of leaves tied together that the Shaman shakes throughout the ceremony. The leaves sound like a waterfall or rushing water, and invoke greater and deeper visions for the patient. The Shaman is responsible for all the people taking Ayahuasca with him. During the ceremony he can read their visions and diagnose their illnesses, and uses these implements according to each situation.

Staring at the Shaman as he fiddled with his pipe, I felt a rush of love for this being that had called me from the mountains to the rainforest, and who believed in me. Love for an old soul that was brave enough to share the ancient knowledge of nature and Ayahuasca with a Westerner. We were beings that had no beginning and no end, intertwined beyond the physical body, part of each other's destiny. I marvelled at how each choice had led me to another, and another, and how each catalyst that had led me to the next place was an interaction with another human being, until I was here, opposite my teacher, the whole process a powerful example of the connections between humans.

"Rebekita, we are ready, *tomar por favor.*" In the glow of the kerosene lamp the Shaman handed me a small plastic beaker, the size of an eggcup. I gingerly took it from him. Staring into the deep red liquid, I smiled despite my fear. The new moon cutting through the night sky meant that this was surely an auspicious time. I nodded to the Shaman. "Ayahuasca, please be kind to me and show me what I need to learn. I am ready to heal and serve and to know who I truly am. Show me the way," I prayed silently, drinking the Ayahuasca in one gulp.

Nothing could have prepared me for the hideous taste of the liquid. Its texture, thick, dark, and heavy, wormed its way down my throat and into my stomach like a long slippery serpent. As it hit my stomach I wanted to vomit, but resisted the urge. My body went cold, the hairs on my arms stood on end, and I involuntarily shuddered. The Shaman looked at me with a large grin on his face while drinking his cup. Even he shuddered. "Well, Rebekita, it is a *dolce* brew, and *fuerte*, yes, we will see what will happen."

The Shaman lit his pipe, sitting with his eyes slightly closed and his back straight. As the blood raced through my veins carrying the Ayahuasca around my body, my muscles began to ache, and I felt the urge to lie down and sleep. Without realising it, I started to slump forward. "Rebekita, sit up straight!" the Shaman barked. I did as I was told, but it took all my effort to remain upright.

After some time, the Shaman blew out the kerosene lamp and we were in darkness. I could no longer keep my eyes open, and my head started to spin. I tried to remain aware of the sensations in my body, but soon my conscious mind began to shut down as my subconscious mind began to awaken.

Then from the darkness the Shaman started to shake the *shacapa* and sing the *Icaro de Ayahuasca*, the *Quechua* chants of the shaman. Suddenly, I felt as if I was hurtling head first down the inside of the body of a huge python. I surrendered to the ups and downs of the serpentine body, having no idea where it would take me. I felt no fear, only exhilaration and a sense of freedom.

Reaching the end of the serpent's shadowy body, I fell into the light and found myself floating in space. A huge condor with wings as wide as the horizon carried me away to another dimension. I looked down and saw Earth, a minuscule planet in the unimaginable vastness of the universe. From this perspective I saw just how small and meaningless our conflicts and wars were. There is another way to live, the condor told me, and my task was to be shown it, and bring it back to the West to share with those who wanted change. The Shaman was now old and there was little time left, so my journey had been speeded up considerably. There was a lot of work to be done as the Shaman's last apprentice.

Then I was back in the present, sitting in the *casita*, aware of the Shaman close to my ear brushing the *shacapa* up and down my body. I saw my mother as I remembered her when I was a little child. She was not really there and yet she looked so real. I felt a huge tug in my lower abdomen where I stored all my emotional baggage as some deep-rooted anger towards her began to stir. Abruptly the anger subsided, and for the first time I saw myself through my mother's eyes. By changing the perspective and seeing myself through her eyes, instead of only seeing her through mine, I realised that the image I held of her was only a reflection of my own needs and wants.

I had not accepted her for who she was as a person, but had fought with her for most of my life, trying to make her live up to my image of a perfect mother. Instead, she had just been herself, though I had never recognised nor accepted this. I couldn't control her and make her a better mother, but by accepting her for who she truly was, without superimposing my own needs and desires onto her, I could start healing the relationship.

Many cultures believe that before we are born our souls choose our parents, in order to help us in our evolutionary growth and to become more loving by learning from their mistakes. It is only our ego that blinds us to these lessons. I realised that I could not wait for my mother to change. Only I, as the daughter, could heal the relationship between us because she had not healed the relationship with her mother, who in turn had not healed the relationship with her own mother, and so on and on into the past. In that moment I felt an immense sense of gratitude for this wonderful woman who had carried me for nine months and given birth to me. She had given me the independence to follow my heart, and had loved me the best way she knew how. I felt a huge urge to give her a hug and spend some real quality time with her, something that I hadn't done in years.

Suddenly, I had the sensation that I was shitting, shitting, shitting, and I could feel and see fireballs coming out of my bottom. I shat until everything had left my lower abdomen and I felt empty. I could see all the shit being burnt up by the eternal fire at the centre of the Earth, by *Pachamama* (the *Quechua* word for Mother Earth). Then I felt a strong need to vomit. Pushing the Shaman aside, I staggered to my knees, and just made it to the balcony before vomiting. Deep guttural retches came from the very core of my being, as red, yellow and brown material was ripped away from me. I felt embarrassed because of the mess I was making, but I couldn't stop throwing up.

Eventually the puking stopped, and I again became aware of chanting and the sound of the shacapa being shaken around my head. Suddenly, another deep retch shook my body, and I was vomiting again. I didn't know if I was real or not, as I left my body and watched from above as the Ayahuasca purged me. My throat was burning, snot was pouring out my nose, and tears were streaming from my eyes, as my body rid itself of all the emotional shit I had allowed to fester. Stuff that I had been holding on to for far too long.

Back in my body, I became aware of the Shaman retching next to me. He turned to me and smiled, and I smiled back as compassion washed over me. I silently thanked the Shaman, feeling more comfortable now that he too was vomiting. As we both stood there leaning over the balcony, the Shaman continued to shake the *shacapa* over my body.

A vision appeared of myself in Machu Picchu, sitting on a rock. White light was bathing me, as a white dove appeared on my hand, and gold flowed from it. Gold dust showered me. A condor appeared at my shoulder and we were flying upwards towards a light that appeared high in the sky. We flew into the light and a feeling of contentment washed over me. Then I was in a bath and lots of little faeries were bathing me with crystal clear water. I felt light and beautiful now that all the negativity had been released from my body.

A beautiful sword and two feminine eyes full of loving kindness appeared in front of me, and I understood that these were gifts to assist me on the journey. The sword was to be used in protection against psychic attack, and the eyes were Knowledge and Wisdom to enable me to see truth. The vision faded, and I was flying alone in the stratosphere. I could again see the Earth, pulsating and dancing in the night sky.

The Shaman was still singing the *icaros*, but they were now much slower. Throughout the ceremony he had continuously shaken the *shacapa* and chanted, except when he was vomiting. Slowly I felt myself returning to the present but could not open my eyes. My body ached all over, and I had no control over my muscles, as everything was numb. The singing finally stopped and all was quiet.

The Shaman lit the kerosene lamp, and eventually I managed to open my eyes to see him staring at me with a big smile on his face. I smiled a little back at him – I was still alive – but only just. I felt physically, emotionally and mentally exhausted with the experience of the ceremony. I wasn't sure who I was anymore. The visions had been so vividly real, and yet I had only moved from my spot when vomiting. I trembled and felt like I wanted to cry, but I did not have the strength to.

The Shaman laughed. "Come Rebekita," he said, pointing in front of him. I could not stand, so crawling on my hands and knees I slowly made my way to the Shaman, and sat in front of him. From his pipe he blew tobacco smoke over my head, body and the space around me until I was covered in a cloud of smoke. "There, that is better, my little *wawita*, now you will sleep well. It has been an important night for you, and you have seen many things, but now it is time for rest. Tomorrow we will talk." I nodded, unable to formulate words.

The Shaman called to Jovino, who came into the room to assist me. He helped me up, but I still could not walk down the steps. Limp and still trembling I slung my arms around his neck and rested my head on his shoulders, breathing in his human smell as he carried me down the ladder. This basic human contact made me feel more real again, and as my feet touched the ground, a bit less numb and empty. I staggered into the darkness to go to the toilet, while Jovino made my bed and prepared the mosquito net for me. I sat squatting under the sparkling night sky, the new moon having sunk into the horizon long before. My mind was a blank and I couldn't grasp anything. My body ached and I just wanted to sleep. Making my way back to the *casita* I heard the Shaman on the other side, also going to the toilet. "Goodnight Don Juanito, and thank you," I whispered into the darkness. "You're most welcome Rebekita," the Shaman replied.

I awoke the next morning feeling that a huge change had taken place. I allowed myself the luxury of laying in my *mosquitero* enjoying this feeling coursing around my body, without worrying what the Shaman was up to. Slowly, I got up, and went to the kitchen *casita* where the Shaman and Pashco were waiting for me with a steaming cup of coffee. I didn't feel hungry or thirsty but the coffee tasted wonderful. I could feel the hot sweet liquid flow down my throat and hit my empty stomach. I sat opposite the Shaman and smiled. He smiled back at me while I sipped the coffee in silence. My brain was still finding it hard to formulate any words, especially in Spanish. I felt disjointed and a bit lost, as if a part of me was missing.

After I had drunk and eaten some yucca, I stood up to go and wash my aching body in the stream, but the Shaman told me that first we would go for a long walk in the rainforest. It was important to digest all the visions and messages received during the ceremony before I cleansed myself of its energy. Grabbing my machete, the Shaman led the way into the Amazon, and it didn't take long before I started to feel more myself again, as I breathed in the richness of the ancient forest.

We had walked a lot in the rainforest together, but I had never before experienced it like I did that morning. Everything seemed so pure, so green and abundantly fertile. No longer lost in thought, I heard noises that I hadn't noticed before. I was in the moment, as if my eyes were open for the first time, and I was actually both seeing *and* feeling the beauty and wonder that surrounded me.

My worries had melted away. I was walking in paradise with the sun warming my body, sensing the invisible rhythmic pulse of nature. I now understood why we walked in silence, instinctively resonating with this powerful, indescribable pulse that pumped through the rainforest, absorbing it into my body. Alive, really alive, and aware of every smell of the lush green foliage, I connected with Mother Nature.

At last the Shaman stopped at Quebrada Limon, a small stream, and after drinking the cool clear water we sat down beside it, watching the little fish swim by.

"So Rebekita, are you well?" the Shaman asked.

"It's funny, but it's as if I am seeing the rainforest for the first time. I feel so connected with everything, animals and plants. Like if I listened carefully enough I could communicate with them."

"It is the heartbeat of Mother Earth you have connected with, for all creatures and humans are part of it. The Ayahuasca showed you many things last night. You are starting to see how everything is connected. The ancient people learned that in order to survive they had to live in harmony with nature. By following this way we have existed for many thousands of years. Humans who live in disharmony are diseased like you. I have never seen anyone vomit so much on their first journey. You are the most unclean person I have ever met. There was lots of negative energy in your soul."

"I can't believe I vomited so much either. I have been doing so much work on myself. I thought that I was comparatively clean," I replied, slightly offended by his comment, although I recognized the truth in it. I felt so different, like a part of me that I was attached to for so long had been vomited out. It was a wonderful feeling of letting go.

"Rebekita, you were not afraid to let go of your pain, and you trusted the journey with the Ayahuasca. The preparation has ended, and the hard training has begun. Ayahuasca will show you many things to help you live with more awareness. For this is the only way to live. We must recognise that we are responsible for everything that is happening in our lives, because we *choose* it. We are creating our greatest dreams and our worst fears simultaneously, whether we know it or not. And our choices come from who we think we are."

"So if I believe I'm a failure, I will create situations in my life where I am always failing. Or if I am always needing approval, I create situations in my life where approval is necessary?" I asked.

"Exactly. We are only free from all limitations when we come from a place of authentic power and unconditional love."

"But how can I tell what is authentic power, and what is power by force?"

"Ahh Rebekita, this is the right question. When your desire is service to others without expecting anything in return, then you are coming from authentic power. When you are controlled by ego, attracted only by selfish needs to make yourself feel better and more powerful, then you are coming from force."

"And what is unconditional love?"

"That you must find for yourself. The key to open this door can only be found as we undertake the journey of life. For this is one of the most important lessons of the journey. To live in unconditional love," the Shaman replied.

The feelings of peace and calm I had been feeling up till then suddenly dissipated as the Shaman's words caused my mind to suddenly flood with doubt and negativity. Authentic power and unconditional love were concepts that I wasn't sure I was ready to explore. But I had agreed to walk this path, and prepared or not, I had to face whatever was necessary. I had to fulfil my destiny and promise to the Shaman, however difficult the journey became.

For most of my life, I had kept myself distracted with external stimulation, busying myself with the daily obstacles of living in the modern world. Now it was time to go to that place deep inside that I had neglected, and explore my own psyche, visit those sleeping volcanoes that I had been afraid of. Ready or not, I was about to go to the core of my truth. I had already started the journey to the Self, and had vomited for most of the Ayahuasca session. I wondered how much more there was left in me.

The Shaman smiled at me. "Come, we should go back to the *casitas*. Pashco will be getting worried, and lunch must nearly be ready." Relieved that the Shaman had broken the silence before my mind got lost completely lost in my thoughts again, we walked back towards the *casitas*. At least I hadn't lost my appetite. I was starving.

After a huge lunch of wild pig soup, rice that we had bought with us from the village, plantain, yucca and *masato*, the Shaman called me into the main *casita*. He was sitting on the floor and he had a little bag in front of him. "Rebekita," he said seriously, "you have taken the first steps on the Shaman's journey. Ayahuasca has been very kind to you for already you have started to see yourself in the mirror of reality. Some Ayahuasca journeys you will find easy, and others more difficult. The way of the Shaman is to accept each day and each moment as you find it. Do not try and control it, but flow with it, knowing that your higher self is guiding you towards becoming who you truly are. I am here to guide you, but I cannot help you. This journey is your journey, and I have to warn you that as you go deeper, the path becomes more difficult and stormy. Soon you will reach a point where your heart and your ego will meet in battle. At this place many people give up, such as Jovino, Walter, and others I have tried to teach. Pepe from the village has reached this point and is now hiding behind alcohol and images of his own importance. His ego is stronger then his heart because his preparations were not solid enough. But you have strong foundations to move past this point. It is not too far away. To help you on your journey I have a gift for you. It is the Shaman's pipe, for you must also learn to be a *tabaquero*. Tobacco from the rainforest has its own properties, and is an essential tool for healing. The smoke of the tobacco helps to purify the energy, and brings visions of spirits. It is used with Ayahuasca to assist the shaman, and you have earned the right to have your own. Remember, Rebekita, a shaman does not possess any supernatural powers, only complete and total faith in the healing energy of '*Dios*'. That is all we need. Ayahuasca is the Mistress, and tobacco is Her servant. With this, and with faith and love the shaman is *buen fuerte*. Use Ayahuasca and the pipe wisely, for it can unlock truth, and that is real power and knowledge."

With that the Shaman handed me the little bag in front of him. Inside was a pipe, with the face of an Indian man beautifully carved into red rainforest wood. I turned to the Shaman with tears in my eyes. All the doubts and negative thoughts I had experienced by the river were gone. My eyes shone. "Thank you," I whispered through my tears, "I will treasure it for the rest of my life."

"Good," said the Shaman in a tone that broke the spell, "now this is a good time to go and take a bath in the stream and clean yourself."

Sitting in the cool stream I tried to find a rational Western framework for the visions I had seen in the Ayahuasca ceremony. But my brain, too overwhelmed by the gift I had just been given, could not register the night before. The pipe was confirmation that Don Juanito believed I had the potential to become a powerful shaman. I already felt more alive and connected then ever, and this was only after the first journey. In the stream I made a decision that however difficult the path would become, I'd smoke the pipe and be reminded of the commitment the Shaman had made to me, and I to him.

By the time I walked back to the *casitas* Pashco and the Shaman had gone to the *chakra* together. Jovino was lying in one of the hammocks dozing in the shade. He opened his eyes and nodded to me, smiling, but had the sensitivity not to ask me how the ceremony went. I could sense the compassion in his eyes. He had walked this path and knew what was going on for me. He understood. Just knowing Jovino was near to me made me feel safe, and most importantly, not alone. Swinging contentedly in the other hammock I recorded my visions and experiences in my diary.

Sometime later Pashco and the Shaman appeared from the large chakra. "Rebekita, tomorrow morning we need to leave here and go back to the village. I've had a vision that some sick people will visit us in the next few days. We leave early tomorrow morning. Your first patients are coming," said the Shaman.

I was shocked. I had only taken one Ayahuasca journey, and already the Shaman wanted me to heal sick people. I wasn't properly prepared. I felt I needed to take at least two or three more Ayahuasca journeys before I did any healing on anyone. This was not how I had planned it. What if I failed? The usual fears were slowly creeping into my mind when the Shaman smiled, seeing the look of horror on my face. "Do not worry Rebekita, we are never given a test we are not ready for. If they are coming so soon, then it is time. Trust the process, and accept that everything is happening perfectly. Believe totally in the boundless healing energy of God, and you will always be able to heal."

With these words I became aware of how my mind constantly reverted to negative thoughts and doubts when something wasn't going the way I hoped it would. I regularly fought with the reality of the situation, instead of accepting that it was all happening perfectly. With this awareness of the workings of my rational mind, I knew I had to stop trying to manipulate the outcome, and start trusting that all experiences were for my highest good.

The next morning, just as we left the centre of the rainforest with the sun rising in the east, a flock of toucans screamed at us from overhead, as though sending a good luck blessing.

\* \* \*

On our arrival home, Pashco began to prepare breakfast. While we were eating, a sick man from the next village down river arrived by canoe with his wife. He was in a lot of pain, complaining about his stomach. Then a woman appeared with her daughter, and another woman with her son from a village even further down the tributary. The Shaman just looked bemused as more people kept turning up throughout the day. "It is good we made so much Ayahuasca, and that it's such a strong brew," he said to me. "We will be busy for the next few days. Prepare yourself, for we will be taking a lot of Ayahuasca."

Once we had settled all the people and their relatives in the main room of the *casita*, the Shaman asked each one of them when they had become sick, and if they thought a *brujo* had put a malicious spell on them. The Shaman made the sick man drink some *chichuwasha* to bring down his fever and chills in preparation for the Ayahuasca ceremony that night.

Later that afternoon, when all the diagnoses had been completed and the patients were comfortable, the Shaman asked me if I wanted to walk to the village with him. I was surprised until I realised it was Sunday, and the only time the Shaman had to meet the other villagers and play some cards. This was a weekly ritual he rarely missed. I was happy to go to the village, as the sight of all the sick people was making me nervous. I wondered if the Shaman expected me to heal all of them, because I wasn't sure that I could. I still had so much to learn.

When we arrived the women were already preparing for their football match. As I approached the pitch one of the girls grabbed me to play on their team. I felt honoured and excited, as this was the first acknowledgment by the village that they were starting to accept me as part of the community, but I was also a little scared. These women took the football match as seriously as the men, and were just as aggressive. Most of them played barefoot, and some were really good.

The game was hard fought and as we neared the end of the exhausting match it was two goals each, and the pressure was on for our side to score the last goal. I was hovering by the goal when the ball miraculously appeared at my feet. Kicking it as hard as I could, it went over the goalkeeper's head and into the back of the net. The girls on my team leapt all over me in celebration. The *gringa loca* could play football too.

Soon after the game I left Don Juanito playing cards, and walked home on my own for the first time, in high spirits. Not only had the Shaman trusted me to go alone, the village was finally accepting me and the winning goal had brought me even closer to them. I was really starting to belong to this secluded community. I was so comfortable and at home here, more than I had ever felt in the West. A fleeting thought skittered across my mind, the possibility that I stay here and never go back, but I didn't allow myself the luxury of entertaining it. I had more important things to think about, like how many people I was going to cure during the ceremony, and anyway, it was improbable that a Westerner could happily live here in the rainforest.

Later that night there were six of us taking Ayahuasca with the Shaman who sat at the head of the circle. There were the three sick people, one of the men that worked on the boat we had taken from Iquitos, and a very drunk Pepe, completed the circle. The Shaman had met Pepe in the village and had insisted he take Ayahuasca with us that night. I could tell that Don Juanito was very angry with Pepe for escaping into the destructive world of alcohol abuse, and even more so for taking Ayahuasca and healing without his supervision. My heart went out to this poor man, as he drunkenly climbed the steps to the main room with as much bravado as he could muster. I could see the fear in his eyes and it scared me, for I knew that this could also happen to me.

The Shaman handed Pepe and I a *shacapa* each, and told us that we had to shake it throughout the ceremony. I was given the first cup of Ayahuasca. Offering up a little prayer of guidance and thanks to the Ayahuasca, I drank the contents in one gulp. Chills ran up and down my spine as the brew snaked its way down my throat and into my stomach. The Shaman refilled the cup and handed it to the woman next to me. The sick woman, on seeing a *gringa* take it so liberally, closed her eyes and swallowed the liquid, her body quietly heaving.

Slowly the cup passed around the circle, each dose carefully measured according to the person taking it. The other sick lady took her dose, and small moans escaped her mouth as she grabbed her husband's hand in reassurance. The man with the sick stomach was next and immediately began retching, but did not puke. The big burly worker from the boat downed his cup and lay on his back, his whole body quivering. Pepe took the brew without hesitation, but to this day I do not know how he physically drank it with so much *traigo* in his body. The Shaman drunk the last cup, and we sat there in the soft warm glow of the kerosene lamp, listening to the sounds of the rainforest outside.

At one point the Shaman blew out the lamp and told Pepe and I to sit up straight and start shaking the *shacapas* as he started to sing the *icaros*. My body desperately wanted to lean against the wall of the casita but I resisted, and begun to do as I was asked, as did Pepe. I entered the serpent's body as I had done in my previous vision. Emerging from the tunnel, a hand gave me a snake, which I received with gratitude. I saw healing spirits enter my body to assist me in the healing process, and received *icaros* in English, realising that each person has his or her own tune. I started to chant and the words just poured out of me until the flow dried up and Pepe took over, singing his own songs. The Ayahuasca then started to communicate with me. Not with words, but with a knowing and an awareness. I was given my first lesson in diagnosing illness.

*Ayahuasca taken by the shaman communicates with the Ayahuasca taken by the sick person, which then guides the shaman to the disease by communicating the patient's pain in the shaman's own body. The shaman then heals the part of the body according to what they feel in their own body. In essence, the shaman becomes a channel to diagnose and find the disease, and then heals it with the healing energy of love. At the same time the shaman must also protect themselves from the negative effects of other people's pain and disease.*

After these messages I felt a little intoxicated, but was still aware of my surroundings. Opening my eyes I saw the Shaman call me to help him heal. Pointing to the balcony I could see the sick man puking violently over the side next to the boatman who was also purging himself of the alcohol binge he had been on the week before. The Shaman was healing one of the sick women, and I could see him leaning over her, sucking her lower abdomen and spitting out the sickness to the side of him. At one point he retched and vomited, as he physically sucked out the disease. Every so often he blew smoke from his pipe over her body and around her head to clear the energy.

I stood next to the sick man, shaking the *shacapa* over his head and stroking his body with the leaves, as the Shaman had done on my first journey, until the man had stopped vomiting. Slowly he sank to his knees and as he slumped there, wasted and worn, I shook the *shacapa* over him and tried to feel his pain in my own body. As I focused, I could feel a sharp stabbing sensation in my own stomach. I did not feel ready to copy the healing technique of the Shaman, so I laid my hands over where I believed the core of his sickness to be, and imagined white healing light entering into him, dissolving the disease. I then blew a smoke cloud around him using my new shaman's pipe, sensing the healing energy of the tobacco smoke.

Meanwhile Pepe, in his drunken state, had managed to destroy his *shacapa* by shaking it too violently. The leaves had gone everywhere; in the Ayahuasca brew, all over the floor, and on the other participants of the ceremony. The place was a mess, but he seemed unaware of what was happening, having spent most of the evening vomiting. The Shaman, ignoring Pepe completely, told me to swap with him, and I went over to the sick woman. Feeling more like a true shaman, I shook the *shacapa* and used my pipe over her too, my heart overflowing with compassion for this woman who was in such obvious distress.

I didn't know where all this love was coming from.

Unexpectedly, the need to heal ached from every pore of my being. As I put my hands over her stomach I saw a white light that turned into a snaking tunnel, and then I shook my *shacapa* over the woman while she vomited for what seemed like ages. I was surprised at the lucidity of my awareness, despite my intoxication. This was very different from my last ceremony where I had only seen visions. This ceremony had shown me how much I desired and wanted to heal and cure these people. I felt so good, virtuous and competent that I did not want it to end.

Eventually, the Shaman relit the kerosene lamp, and slowly we all started to return to our ordinary senses. It had been a long night and we were all exhausted, especially the Shaman, who staggered to his feet and immediately went into his own bedroom. The rest of us stayed in the main house, and it did not take long for everyone to unpack their mosquiteros and settle down.

I could not sleep as my head was whirling with the ceremony. I had actually healed while under the influence of Ayahuasca and it had felt so good. I was convinced the Shaman was really proud of me. I hadn't been drunk, or destroyed the *shacapa* like Pepe; the fallen apprentice. I had proved myself a serious and diligent student. Ayahuasca obviously wanted to work through me, otherwise so many sick people would not have come to us so soon. Feeling restless with excitement for the future, and unable to lie still, I crept among the silhouettes of sleeping bodies and sat out on the porch, watching the night sky. There were hundreds of shooting stars falling to earth, and I could feel the power of the great universe reflecting what I was feeling. I was no longer a failure.

\* \* \*

The next morning I awoke feeling terribly vulnerable, the smile no longer on my face. I felt cut loose and adrift on a wild and stormy sea, consumed with anger and frustration, but I didn't know its source, or at what moment in time this feeling had started. I had fallen asleep so blissfully happy but I was now overpowered and overwhelmed by these dark feelings.

The sick people were still groaning and ill. They had not been instantaneously healed as I had expected, and suddenly I doubted this path, Don Juanito's effectiveness as a shaman and teacher, and ultimately, myself. For if he was the powerful healer that I thought he was, and if I was the diligent and successful apprentice that I thought I had been, then all the people would have been cured. I started to question over and over whether Don Juanito was a charlatan. I was ashamed of these feelings that I had about him, and something deep within me was desperately resisting seeing him. I didn't trust myself not to say something terrible.

The night before was forgotten as the anger poured out of me and I felt as though I was falling into an abyss. Avoiding the sick people, I was able to sneak out without being seen by anyone and went to the river to try and calm my crazy mind. Sitting by the flowing water I tried to work out where this anger had come from. Fear clouded my brain and the storm I had felt brewing in my mind erupted. "*Run.*" It was screaming at me. "Get out of this place before you go any further. You don't need to be here. Find another teacher, one that will take you on a path that isn't this hard. There are many, but leave this place. *Go Now.*"

And as I sat by the river I realised that the anger with the Shaman was only really an extension of my anger towards myself. Maybe I really was the failure that I had always believed myself to be. I was scared, seeing the crystal image I had built from my expectations about myself start to crack and break, and the truth reveal itself. I knew the Shaman would be able to see the real me too, and maybe he would change his mind, reject me and break my heart. I began to panic as I realised I could no longer escape from the real me. And I could no longer hide the real me from the Shaman.

I had arrived at the impasse that all apprentices must overcome, the battle between the ego and the heart. But I was tired of running away from myself and blaming other people for my suffering. This was the opportunity to stop escaping, and confront my deepest fears. To own, and take responsibility for everything that was happening in my life. I had to lose sense of who I *thought* I was, and accept who I *truly* was, the dark and the light, and then I could consciously choose which path I wanted to follow – the path of love or the path of fear.

But was I strong enough to let go of my fear and complete the apprenticeship?

## CHAPTER TEN

### *Ego or Heart?*

*I was really scared. A tidal wave was coming towards us. I tried to run from it, find a high place, but there was none. I was trapped. I couldn't escape. I was going to die. And then I awoke.*

I had reached the impasse just like every apprentice before me, and I felt so alone. I had completely lost all sense of identity. The structures, organisations, family, friends, rules, regulations and images that ordinarily defined me did not exist here. In some sense I was completely free to be whatever and whomever I desired. The problem was that I didn't know how to redefine myself. I still did not know who I truly was. I only knew what I was not.

There was no one to turn to who could explain it all in a way I could understand. Even the Shaman seemed so far away from me, too busy healing the sick people that had come to us to give me any attention. Pashco was busy cooking and attending to the visitors, although most of the time she kept out of my way. I did not know what to do to be useful, and this just intensified my feelings of vulnerability, and fuelled my doubts.

I also felt starved of affection, and desperately wanted a hug or some physical contact to make me feel human again. I missed Harry, and yearned to feel his arms around me, protecting me, but there was no way of contacting him to hear his words of reassurance, no way of knowing whether he was still waiting for me and loved me, regardless of whether I failed or succeeded. He was now too far away from me, physically, mentally and spiritually. As all these insecurities and needs began to build up within me, I didn't know how to release the tension and frustration.

That afternoon the Shaman and I went fishing. It was a welcome escape from the infirmary that had become our home, and the perfect opportunity to talk to the Shaman about what I was feeling before the ceremony that night. Once on the river I tried to let my worries ebb away as I allowed the soothing sound of oar on water to lull my mind into a state of calmness. Being alone with the Shaman, as teacher and apprentice, my isolation seemed less intense.

We reached a secluded place upstream, away from the last few houses, and threw our lines into the water. I let the sun warm my body and everything started to seem much brighter and clearer. I just needed a sign, something to reassure me that I was on the right path, and that I really had the potential to be a healer and shaman.

Suddenly a thought came to me, and I quickly convinced myself that if I caught the first fish I would know for sure that everything was happening perfectly. I would be back in control and maybe then I would stop questioning everything, and really start trusting. But I had set myself up because the Shaman caught the first fish. And not just any fish but a huge Sangero, a rare fish to catch, considered a delicacy in these parts. I felt myself going into panic as it hit me that I was not in control of anything. I couldn't manifest everything at will just because I wanted it to happen like that. Which meant that I had to let go of my doubt and start really trusting that it was all happening perfectly even if it was not exactly how I thought it should be.

"Rebekita, you see what we can create when we have the right intention. Now we can feed all the sick people with this fish.

Everything is working in harmony," the Shaman said in satisfaction. Then he took one look at my face and recognised the storm brewing deep within me.

"Is something wrong? You look angry."

As he spoke I could feel myself starting to boil with all the deep suppressed frustration at the lack of control I had over life. I was trying so hard to get it right and just *be*, but it was proving useless, and I couldn't stop the torrent of emotion triggered by the Shaman's words.

"I feel so confused. So lost. I don't know what I am doing here in the rainforest. I do not belong. I am a Westerner, born and bred in London. How could I have even considered taking on this apprenticeship? I must have been mad. I have come so far and yet I have so far to go, and for what? Why am I doing this? No one seems to want to embark on this journey and I don't blame them. This is so difficult it's almost impossible. There has to be an easier way. I mean, how can I realistically let go of everything I have been taught to believe and just trust my heart? Its crazy to even think it is possible. Nothing seems real anymore. I don't know who I am anymore. I am losing my mind, Don Juanito, I am losing my fucking mind," I ranted as tears flowed down my face.

The Shaman gave me a look that was filled with compassion, and with a small smile on his face, relit his pipe. He put his hand on my head and blew tobacco smoke over my head and around my body while chanting some *icaros*. Immediately, I felt my pain dissolving and a peaceful flow of energy began to soar through my body.

"Rebekita, you have reached the point that many cannot pass. There is nothing you can do to make it easier. This is the time when the apprentice must descend into the abyss of trust and faith. Only then can we see the magic of a perfect world all around us. How long you will be in this place it is impossible to say. For some apprentices it can be many years, for others weeks and for others only days. This is the most important of all the tests for the apprentice. Many do not have the patience or the strength to follow their hearts and trust moment by moment without giving up. The sign of a true shaman, whether living in the Amazon rainforest or living in the urban jungle, is to trust that things are going to plan, and to have even greater trust when things are not as you would like them to be. Only then do we live a life without suffering."

"But Don Juanito, how do I know it's all going to plan when things feel like they are going so wrong and everything is falling apart. How can I trust a process when there is no tangible evidence that all is working perfectly?"

"Ah, Rebekita, do not forget it is our hearts that are pure in motive and in spirit. It is our minds that are infected with our wants and needs. Only when we truly follow our hearts can we accept every moment, even if we think and judge with our rational minds that it is not right."

"But sometimes I do not know the difference between my desires, needs and wants," I hiccupped through my tears.

"All you need to do is decide who you want to be and then listen to the small voice within you that will lead you on the path to achieving that goal. Trust that voice within you and you will be given what you need. You are already on the path Rebekita, and you are closer than you think to knowing this wisdom. But there is danger ahead, for now the ego will fight to maintain its superiority. Pepe is one whose ego has controlled him and he is using *traigo* as his escape. He is no longer walking the path, and I can no longer teach him. Do not give up Rebekita, *falter tiempo*, be strong, and you will overcome this impasse," he added sadly.

"I promise you I will not let you down and I will not turn to alcohol," I replied confidently, although a flittering of fear scuttled down my back. I had used alcohol as an escape for years and I wasn't about to fall back into that trap now.

We fell into silence and slowly my mind calmed down as I

began to feel more relaxed about everything, especially when I ended up catching more fish than the Shaman. I had come too far to let the Shaman down now even though I felt further away from the goal than ever.

We paddled home, the canoe weighty with fish and the setting sun turning the sky a beautiful blend of oranges, pinks, mauves and reds. I breathed in deeply the sweet scent of dusk, and tried to connect with the wholeness and rhythmic flow of nature, despite my feelings of separation. As I heard the birds deep within the rainforest shrieking to each other I knew that if I wanted to become the shaman I knew I had the potential to be, I really needed to let go. Let go of my need to heal. Let go of getting it right. Let go of worrying about failing. Let go of becoming a shaman. Let go of the need for the Shaman's constant approval and the need to prove myself. I just had to *let go*.

When we returned from the river the two women had left feeling much better, taking various herbs and potions that Pashco had prepared for them. I let out a huge sigh of relief. It was the sign I had been looking for that the Shaman really was a powerful healer, and that everything was happening perfectly, even when I could not see it. That night there were only four of us for Ayahuasca, the Shaman, the sick man, Walter, and me. While we were relaxing, waiting for the Shaman to appear from his bedroom, Walter told me that he had wanted to learn under the tutelage of the Shaman and had taken Ayahuasca many times. He had gone far in the apprenticeship but having reached this impasse, couldn't go beyond it and had rejected the path. He hadn't been able to even smell Ayahuasca without retching for years, and all the insights and power that he had acquired during his apprenticeship had now been lost. I nodded my head in sympathy but immediately felt fearful. I didn't know why he had mentioned the story, but I sensed that the same thing could easily happen to me. The fearful feeling dissolved and was replaced by a need to prove to Walter that I was special, and

169

courageous enough to overcome this impasse.

When the Shaman passed me the cup, for the first time I felt an indescribable fear about taking Ayahuasca. I wasn't sure why I suddenly felt like this, but then I remembered that both Jovino and Walter had warned about this moment when the apprentice becomes so fearful of the Ayahuasca that it takes all their strength to drink the brew. It is the ego's last trick to entice the apprentice away from the path. The only way through the fear is to face it, and I was sure that I had reached this place so quickly because of the insights I had received that afternoon.

As the Shaman poured the Ayahuasca into the cup he smiled at me and I felt so honoured to be his apprentice. There was real love in his eyes, and I realised that maybe I was also the daughter he had never had. My reciprocal love for him gave me the strength to drink the Ayahuasca, despite every cell, every muscle, every fibre of my being, screaming *NO!* I had to be strong and not allow the fear to triumph.

"Please do not reject me. Please help me to be a powerful and successful healer so I can help people and be of service," I prayed. My heart felt strong. In this ceremony I was going to prove to the Shaman that I could overcome any impasse.

I drank the liquid in one gulp. This time my whole body began to crawl with revulsion as it snaked down my throat. I wanted to throw it back up immediately, and it took all my effort to keep the liquid in my stomach as I retched a few times. The thought that maybe the Ayahuasca was starting to reject me flitted into my mind, and I tried to ignore it as I felt the panic rise. I didn't know whether I had enough strength or courage to overcome the fear, but I had already drunk the brew and now all I could do was accept whatever was going to happen to me.

The cup was passed around and soon the Shaman had blown out the kerosene lamp. We sat in darkness waiting for the Ayahuasca to start speaking to each of us, to show us who we truly were. The Shaman thrust the *shacapa* in my hand and starting to shake it, I entered the snake's body. This time as I journeyed through the serpent tunnel, I felt terrible, as if my body was falling apart. Without warning, the vision of the snake disappeared and I was back in the ceremony. I was acutely aware of my surroundings, and there was clarity to the darkness and the shapes of the other bodies.

Then in the darkness the veil between our world and the spirit world dissolved and I could see spirits around the group, especially around the sick man and the Shaman. It seemed normal to see the spirits and I wasn't afraid or fearful of them. I could sense them near me and I heard whispering in my ear, telling me that the Shaman was one of the last authentic and powerful healers existing on the planet who can heal with universal love. The voices said that I needed to trust him completely in order to overcome the fear and complete the apprenticeship.

I looked over at the Shaman as he sucked the sick man's stomach, spitting out the illness, but something stopped me from going over to assist him in the healing. I couldn't move, and ached all over. I could barely find the co-ordination and control to shake the *shacapa*, and the songs did not come to me. Halfway through the ceremony the Shaman came over and offered me a cup of something, but I was unsure if it was a vision or reality. I shook my head and pushed his hands away, scared it might have been a *brujo* disguised as the Shaman, and I refused until he said "*Tomar!* " in a voice that I could not disobey. I drank the liquid, which tasted like *El Camphor*, and was immediately overwhelmed by fear. I began retching and vomiting over the side of the balcony.

I slid to my knees in exhaustion but the fear had passed, and as I sat back in the circle I saw a pack of wolves pass by me. A beautiful big owl with huge eyes came to me. He took me on his back to a planet that had all the species of animals and plants that had ever existed in the universe. Everything was so healthy, lush and fertile, perfectly formed and full of vitality, pulsating and vibrating with light, every atom and molecule existing with awareness at every moment. Love poured from every living cell in the Garden of Eden. Humans were living in total harmony with the planet and every living thing upon her. War did not exist because there was nothing to fight for. Nothing belonged to the humans who lived there. They were only stewards, protecting and caring for this paradise.

Then the vision changed and I saw the Earth, our home. I saw the environmental destruction that is affecting our oceans, forests, meadows, deserts and mountains. I saw the spiritual pollution that has allowed humans to continue to suffer from malnutrition, disease, starvation, injustice and poverty. I saw the emotional pollution, as the divergence between the rich and poor gets wider. And I saw the mental pollution as we create enemies in order to feed the fire of fear and control.

The vision shifted again and I saw that the outer pollution was only a reflection of our own inner malaise. I felt a black weight of despair on my heart as the owl told me that human beings have created systems of belief and patriarchal mythologies that have led us astray from our true purpose as a collective race of beings on this planet. Living in disharmony without following the natural rhythms of life has created a world that festers with fear, disease, misery and despair. "What have we done?" I screamed out. "We are destroying paradise."

"Do not be distressed," the owl told me. "There is still hope. Mother Earth is now ready to realise the vision she has for herself. She is ready to transmute to the next stage of her evolution. The vision that you have just seen is to be the home for those humans who have decided to continue living in fear and greed. The first vision is the new Earth for those who choose love instead of fear, light instead of dark, awareness instead of ignorance, cooperation instead of conflict, power instead of force, peace instead of war. It is for those that have decided to follow the path of unconditional love. This is a vision of our possible future."

Then I was back in the Ayahuasca ceremony. I could still see the spirits, but there seemed to be fewer around us. Everyone had stopped vomiting and the Shaman was still chanting the songs, but they were less intense now. I felt I had been gone a long time, and a momentary feeling of guilt welled up about not helping the Shaman with the healing. Concentrating on the icaros the feeling disappeared and my body filled with light, weightless, as if it did not belong to me. Soon the energy dissipated and the last of the spirits left us. The Shaman stopped chanting and we sat in silence and darkness for a while. After some time, the Shaman lit the kerosene lamp and the orange glow again filled the room.

The Shaman got up, and without giving me a second glance or saying goodnight he went to his room. I sensed that he was upset with me for not participating in the healing part of the ceremony, and the usual tape started to play in my head that maybe I had let him down. Before I drank the Ayahuasca I had promised myself that I was going to prove I could overcome the impasse and be a diligent apprentice. Instead I had got so caught up in the visions I had not assisted the Shaman in any way. I felt ashamed with myself and his silence only compounded my guilt. I forgot about my visions of the earth and seeing the spirits for the first time. They seemed so much less important when compared to the healing aspects of the ceremony. Settled under my *mosquitero* my mind raced over the events of the night until I fell into a troubled sleep.

The next morning I awoke very late feeling ill. My head and body ached and I could not stop crying, but at least this time I knew why. I was still so attached to the image that I was the Shaman's most special apprentice, and I desperately needed his approval to assure me that this was the truth. Because I had not assisted in the ceremony I was afraid the Shaman was angry with me.

I could hear Pashco and Doily, laughing and joking in the kitchen. Reluctantly, I left the safety of my *mosquitero* and wandered in to join them. Both of them ignored me and continued to prepare smoked fish. I sat down, staring out at the river, feeling very sorry for myself.

"Ah, here she is at last," said Doily. "The fake shaman has finally woken up."

On hearing her words my whole world collapsed, as the illusory image of myself as a powerful healer shattered yet again. Even Doily, who was only eight, thought I was a fake. I began to cry, exhausted from trying to hold on to an image that was constantly being destroyed by other people.

Pashco turned, and taking one look at me, told me to take my clothes off. She then bathed my head and body in *El Camphor*, while blowing on me and chanting some *icaros*. Immediately the aches in my head and pains in my body disappeared. I went to bathe in the river and felt much better. With my mind clearer, I knew it had been immature of me to allow Doily's comments to make me feel insecure, and was able to recognise it as jealousy. Time had been cruel to Doily, who desperately wanted to become the Shaman's apprentice, but she was too young, and the Shaman would be too old to teach her when she came of age.

I wandered slowly back to the house. It was empty. The sick man had awoken feeling much better, and had also gone back to his own village with some herbs the Shaman had prepared for him, while Pashco had gone to the *chakra* to find Don Juanito. As I climbed the steps, relieved to be alone, I could see Jovino swinging in the hammock and my heart gave a little leap of happiness. I hadn't seen him in what seemed like ages. He had been working at the tourist lodge further up the river as a guide, and was very busy. At last I could speak to someone who could really understand all my doubts, worries and fears. I had kept everything in for so long and Jovino was the only person I knew who would give me the advice I needed. He always appeared just at the right moment.

I sat in the opposite hammock and greeted Jovino, who opened his eyes in surprise, and on seeing me his beautiful Indian face broke into a big smile.

"So Rebekita, you are here. I was hoping to see you. I am sorry I have not been around to catch up, but I have been really busy working at the tourist lodge. I want you to know that I have been thinking about you a lot, and Pashco has updated me on what is happening."

"Oh Jovino, I am so happy to see you. This morning I couldn't stop crying until Pashco bathed me in *El Camphor*, and now I feel a bit better. Things have been really difficult recently and sometimes I feel so confused and afraid. I am no longer sure of who I am or what is real and what isn't. I have seen some amazing things in the visions, and assisted in healing, but mostly I feel like I'm taking one step forward and two steps back, and wonder if I will ever reach the goal, " I blurted out, the words tumbling out of my mouth like a waterfall after a storm.

"Yes, I know that you have been having some difficulty. Pashco told me that you have reached the impasse. I know how you feel for I too tried to walk the path of the shaman, but I could not go beyond this point. Even now I cannot talk about the experience because I nearly lost my mind. But you are strong Rebekita, and courageous, and loving and special. You will go beyond the impasse. I knew it the moment I met you. You are different. You will find your way." Jovino said.

"Thank you for believing in me. I've missed you. I've missed your support and companionship. Sometimes I feel like I am going mad not being able to talk about my experiences with anyone who can understand," I said before I could stop myself, consumed with a feeling of relief that he understood. Emotional outbursts like this were not common in the rainforest.

In that moment electricity passed between us that was highly charged with passion, as though an unseen build up of energy was about to explode. Staring at him I saw just how beautiful he was, with his chocolate-coloured skin smooth and supple, his big slanted eyes, his high cheekbones, small nose and beaming smile. I noticed how his thick mop of black hair fell around his face, and the strength of his body, muscles protruding through his white t-shirt, his smooth, hairless skin glowing with health and vitality. I knew he was seeing me for the first time too. Jovino broke the tension. "Rebekita, do you want to go for a walk in the rainforest? It will clear your head and make you feel better," he said, looking straight at me with a twinkle in his eyes.

"Great idea. Let's go," I said immediately, almost breathless with anticipation.

We both leaped off the hammocks and, grabbing our machetes, we took a different path than the one leading to the *chakras*. We both knew we did not want to meet the Shaman and Pashco on the way, and plunged into the dark green foliage. We walked in silence, I following Jovino, as we went deeper into the rainforest along a route I did not know. Without warning he stopped and, standing beneath the boughs of a great tree that had been standing for millennia, Jovino grabbed me, kissing me full on the lips.

His lips tasted salty, sweet and human. My arms snaked around his neck and soon we were hugging and kissing with intensity and a passion that surprised me, while the energy of the rainforest only fuelled the fire. We couldn't control ourselves. Jovino's hands were all over me, feeling my breasts, my buttocks, my arms and legs, not tenderly, but with a soft urgency that aroused me even more.

We ripped our t-shirts off and our skins touched, sending me into a spiral of ecstasy. Smelling of the rainforest, his body danced, glistening with sweat, sending out raw undiluted passion. I had never experienced anything like it before, and was already addicted. His rough hands explored my breasts and then he fell to his knees, pulling me down with him, and took each breast delicately into his mouth. My hands played with his hair as I looked up at the tall tree that towered above us. It was as if the tree's vitality was adding to our ecstatic fervour.

The Shaman's son licked his way down to my jeans and tore them off. I was naked and vulnerable, my body shaking with anticipation. Tugging his trousers off he leaned against the tree. I moaned as he lifted me up and gently slid into me. We started to move in rhythm, the sounds of the rainforest receding into the background. I felt him inside me and shivers of bliss ran up and down my spine. I was human again as we made love, with the rainforest urging us on faster and faster. We both slipped into the rhythm of nature, of fertility, of life. Little moans of joy escaped from our lips as our bodies merged together. We became one, climaxing together, the tree a silent witness to our lovemaking.

Slowly he withdrew, and still naked we just hugged and caressed each other as the world came back into focus. The urgency had gone, and now we had time to explore each other's bodies. Reluctantly we pulled apart and dressed. Every part of me felt alive, body, mind and spirit. Jovino had saved me from almost certain madness. I felt grounded and everything had perspective once again. We were both glowing, and looking at me he smiled that special smile, taking my hand and lovingly kissing it.

Jovino broke the spell between us. "We'd better go back as they will be wondering where we are. It is getting late and lunch will be ready," he said, turning to the sun to check its position in the sky. He headed off into the rainforest and after a few metres stopped at a tall palm tree. After analysing its position and walking around it for a few minutes, he started chopping it with his machete. I stood and watched in surprise. After about five minutes of striking the skinny trunk, the tree started to topple and with a little extra push crashed to the ground.

"Come Rebekita, we will have *chonta* for lunch today," shouted Jovino from the head of the tree. I walked over to him and saw that he was cutting out the tender white flesh in the middle of the palm tree, the heart of palm.

"Have you tasted this? We don't eat it much in the rainforest because we think it's tasteless, but all Westerners seem to like it. Pashco will prepare it with some *cocona* from our *chakra* for you." I couldn't believe that Jovino had chopped down a tree that had been growing for years just so that I could eat its heart. No wonder heart of palm was so expensive in the supermarkets in the West.

We arrived back at the house, and the Shaman and Pashco were waiting for us to eat lunch. The Shaman stared at us questioningly but we acted like nothing had happened. Jovino ate quickly and disappeared. I watched him go to Lydia and Walter's *casita* with a sense of longing I had not experienced since I had left Harry and come to Peru.

I was silent, as I only half listened to the Shaman talk about the *chakra* and the work that needed to be done, reliving the experience with Jovino again and again. My body still glowed with his touch and I felt like a sexy, desirable woman. Warm shivers of energy flowed around my body as I remembered the orgasm I had experienced. It had brought me back from the brink of the abyss, and I again felt warm and safe and blissfully happy. This was real. I was back in touch with my self, no longer alone, no longer the Shaman's apprentice. I was now Jovino's lover, an identity I could understand and relate to.

I began to imagine myself marrying Jovino and living next to the Shaman in a *casita* we had built from rainforest materials, where he and I would heal together, and Jovino would hunt and fish, providing the food for our family. I could teach English to some of the villagers so that they would be employable as guides for the tourist lodge. We would live happily ever after, an uncomplicated and safe life, with no electricity, television, computer, radio, or anything 'modern.' I would be with a man who understood this path and the obstacles I would encounter, and he would be able to support me.

Then my thoughts were flooded with images of sweet, caring Harry who was waiting patiently for me back in the West. Harry, who supported and loved me unconditionally, whatever I decided to do and whatever path I chose to walk.

After lunch the Shaman, Pashco and I went back to the *chakra* to plant *sandia* seeds. It was good to be able to do physical work and keep my mind busy. Once I got into the rhythm of planting I remembered the vision I had experienced of Mother Earth in all her glory. This was the same vision and message that the Shaman had also seen and I realised that Ayahuasca could communicate on both an individual and collective level. The visions I had seen were communications for the collective rather than just for me as an individual. The vision of Mother Earth in the fullness of her beauty was real and all we needed was for humanity to believe it and bring it into reality.

That night the mosquitoes were brutal, and we were all under our *mosquiteros* early. The Shaman looked tired after all the healing he had done. I hoped that Jovino would come to my mosquitero in the middle of the night, but he didn't, and a little part of me was relieved. This man had consumed my thoughts all afternoon. I was here to learn how to be a shaman, and now I had fallen in love.

# CHAPTER ELEVEN

## *Beyond the Impasse*

*The sky was grey and stormy and the flood was almost upon us. There was an oppressive energy and tension in the air, full of fear for the unknown, and I did not know how to best prepare myself for the coming deluge. I was consumed by dread of the impending tidal wave and the destruction it would bring with it. All I could do was trust that 'Dios es Grande'. And then I awoke.*

After that day in the rainforest, Jovino and I secretly embarked on a passionate affair that was dangerous and exciting. However, we were playing with fire. The Shaman was very possessive of me, and I sensed that he would be angry and disappointed if he knew. I was also concerned that if he found out he would terminate the apprenticeship, but I could not stop. I only felt real when I was in Jovino's arms. When we were alone we could not keep our hands off each other, consumed by the blazing passion that was between us and, although I felt more human, I also felt much weaker.

I was obsessed, and even when Jovino was not around, could not concentrate on the apprenticeship, and ached for him desperately. Our friendship lay in tatters, because I was no longer able to confide in him about what I was going through; Jovino had now become the source of my confusion. One moment I was happy, contented and blissful, and then I would feel guilty about the sex and fantasies that constantly occupied my thoughts. There was no commitment, no plans, no open displays of affection, and after our sexual encounters Jovino would disappear, leaving me feeling empty and alone, longing for Harry's arms around me, to hold and save me.

Hours would pass like days as I waited for Jovino to come back from the tourist lodge. I knew he did not love me as Harry loved me, and yet I did not know why I needed him so much, or why this urge for him was so overpowering, when the reason I was in the rainforest was to learn with the Shaman. After a while I was no longer clear about what I wanted. I thought I wanted Jovino with me all the time, to make our relationship known, to commit to each other. Then I would spend time with the Shaman and was reminded of my promise to myself.

I was taking Ayahuasca three nights a week, walking in the rainforest, fishing or just being together, the Shaman and his apprentice, and during those times I was closer than ever to a true understanding of myself. Soon, the secrecy and the pressure of straddling two worlds - the world of the physical with Jovino, and the world of Shamanism with Don Juanito - made me feel angry towards Jovino and guilty about my lack of commitment to the shaman's path. I didn't know how to escape the predicament I had created for myself.

Just as events began to take their toll and I was really starting to lose my sanity, Don Juanito decided that it was time for us to return to *El Centro*. He wanted to plant more medicinal plants, sow maize and to take Ayahuasca again, this time with the whole family. I was very happy with this decision. I needed to get away from the village, and I knew the peace and calm of *El Centro* would help me sort out my feelings.

The morning was spent organising everyone who was going that day, and those who would come for the big Ayahuasca ceremony the next evening. Pepe, Jovino, Walter, Elsa, Ramon and I sat around chatting while chaos ensued. I knew I was in love with Jovino, watching him talking and laughing. He was the most beautiful, sexy and exotic man I had ever met, and when I saw him look over at me I hoped he felt the same way about me. We tried to avoid eye contact but my infatuation was impossible to hide. I couldn't wait for the next night. It was my opportunity to show him how close I was to becoming a powerful shaman and healer.

As the sun hit the highest part of the sky, we were ready to leave in one canoe: Elsa, Ramon, Esther and the baby, Elsa and Esther's brother Harly, the Shaman, Pashco, and I, three dogs, four chickens, a sack of fish, rice, coffee, and all our bedding and clothes. I enjoyed the warm glow of belonging laughing with the others by the side of the river, as the Shaman tried to coerce the dogs into the canoe.

We were in the middle of the dry season and from the river we needed to walk about fifty minutes across the rainforest to the *casitas*. We tied up the canoe at the bank of the river, where a path snaked its way into the rainforest. I had to carry my rucksack on my back, and another huge bag with all my bedding around my shoulders because I still refused to sleep on the floor like everyone else. Despite the extra weight, the foam mattress was a luxury I was not willing to give up. The sack of fish was balanced precariously on top of the rucksack. It really tested my endurance but I had to prove to myself that I was one of the rainforest people, for we were all overloaded with bags and sacks.

Although the walk was challenging I was surprised at my own stamina. All the hard work in the *chakras* was paying off and I was able to fall into a silent meditation, connecting to the pulse of the rainforest as it urged me on. We all reached the *casitas* in good time, and I was sweating profusely as I slumped onto the cool wooden floor. Ramon, who had carried the most cargo, had arrived first. I always marvelled at his strength and stamina. He was like superman, loping through the rainforest as if it was a stroll in the park. Smiling with compassion, he handed me a bowl of *masato*. Gulping down the cool creamy liquid I soon felt refreshed and energised.

Pashco and I walked to the stream that ran by the house and filled up two buckets each with water, which we carried back. Pashco then began cleaning the kitchen *casita* and I went over to the largest *casita* to unpack my bags and find a sleeping space. Ramon, Elsa, Harley and Esther were sharing the third, smaller *casita*. It took a while to sort everything out but finally we had organised the sleeping arrangements.

Ramon went hunting, Elsa, Harley and Esther sat playing cards, Pashco started to prepare the sack of fish for supper, and Don Juanito and I went to find Ayahuasca to prepare for the following night's ceremony. My heart sang, as it always did when we went walking into the rainforest together. Without Jovino around to distract me I was once again the Shaman's dedicated apprentice.

I always felt honoured to be participating in this ancient ritual of apprentices preparing Ayahuasca with their teacher, a tradition that has been passed down for thousands of years. We walked to the same part of the rainforest where we had found the Ayahuasca last time. Rummaging around under the foliage the Shaman uncovered some very old Ayahuasca vine and, as he told me they were very potent, I felt a shiver of anticipation run down my spine. I had a strong sense that tomorrow's ceremony was going to be very significant.

After we had harvested enough, we put the Ayahuasca into our sack together with the visionary leaves, and sat under a tree. The Shaman chanted *icaros* to thank the spirits that guarded the Ayahuasca and kept it safe, and as he chanted I remembered sitting under this same tree, the first time we had collected Ayahuasca together all those moons ago. I saw how far I had come and how much I had learnt since then. Suddenly realising how close I was to becoming a powerful shaman, I felt impatient for the next night, knowing that this ceremony would prove it.

"Rebekita," the Shaman said, calling me out of my reverie. "You must never worry about money. Let go of it, and when you need it *Dios* will provide. The more you give the more you will receive."

"Shaman, I know all that. I lost my pouch, remember, and I still stayed here even though I had no documents or money. I *have* let go of money." I said, indignantly.

"If that is the case you will not mind giving Doily some money. Next week there are elections for this year's *Primavera Queen*. We have to raise a certain amount of money so that we can buy her a new dress, shoes and other things, and we are about forty soles short. This is nothing for you, but for her it is everything. This is the last year she can ever be the *Primavera Queen*, for next year she goes to school in Iquitos."

Then I realised that despite all I had been shown I had not let go of money because I *did* mind that he had asked me, and now I was in a dilemma. When I had lost my money pouch I had to let go of it, but now that it had been found I was again attached to it. I had been giving out money to Jovino, the Shaman, and Walter whenever they asked for it, albeit somewhat reluctantly, and now I only had ninety soles left. Maybe I would need to buy batteries, more tapes, or cigarettes, and I also needed money for emergencies. There was also the cost of travel back to Iquitos by boat - thirty soles for the Shaman, Pashco and I. After much deliberating I decided that I couldn't give forty soles to Doily. Instead I decided to give her twenty soles, and pay for Don Juanito and Pashco's return ticket from Iquitos to the village. I felt comfortable with this decision, and more in control as it meant I had some spare money just in case something went wrong.

"I do not have forty soles to give to Doily. I can give her twenty soles, but I must have some spare for an emergency. I know *Dios es Grande*, but how does that provide for me in the rainforest?" I replied.

"Whatever you can give it is your choice but remember, do not live for the future. You do not know what will happen next. When you live in the now, the future takes care of itself." His words made me feel a little guilty. I didn't know whether I was being stingy or prudent.

"Rebekita, we will have no more talk of money," said the Shaman, breaking the tension in the atmosphere. "I have bought you a cigarette as I thought you may want one, and you always forget to bring yours," the Shaman added with a smile. Taking the cigarette, love and gratitude swelled in my heart for my teacher sitting beside me. He knew me so well, and could read my mind and my intentions. We were so connected, he and I. Sitting in silence, we smoked the cigarettes, taking in the rainforest sounds and movement around us. I loved this place.

Despite what the Shaman said, as we walked back my mind replayed the conversation about money we had just had, and I hoped I had made the right decision. "But," the voice inside me said, "Where is your trust and your faith that everything will be provided for you? You are still holding on to the need to control your environment. Let go and you will be protected."

I was surprised at just how loud and clear this voice was. I was being tested yet again, but this was not the same as losing my pouch. Then I had no control over the situation, and could only accept the loss of my money. If I was to live the Shaman's way, I needed to trust that by giving it away I would not be short myself, and accept that there is always enough. I was really starting to experience this, but it seemed so much harder to accept when money was involved. After mulling over the dilemma in my mind for ages, I decided to wait and see what happened.

After supper of fresh *majass* soup, Elsa, Ramon, Esther, Harley and I played cards while the Shaman and Pashco had some time together in their *mosquitero*. Not long into the card game the wind picked up and started to whisk the leaves and dust across the ground around the *casitas*. In the distance, streaks of lightening flared and thunder could be heard exploding from far away. A wild storm was coming towards our part of the rainforest. Quickly we ensured everything was safely covered and in a dry place, and that the leaves of the *casitas* were secure. A few hours later the storm reached us, wild and raging, clearing the energy for tomorrow's ceremony.

The next morning the Shaman and I were up at daybreak, preparing the brew. We took it in turns to splinter the pieces of Ayahuasca, and lay them in the cauldron. Once the Ayahuasca was on the fire, Don Juanito and Ramon went fishing. We were expecting Gordo (a friend from the village), Pepe, Jovino, Walter, Lydia, Eric and Doily to join us for the ceremony, and we all needed to be fed the next morning. Pashco looked after the fire while I went to collect more firewood from the *chakra*, carrying a bundle of logs on my shoulders that I hoped would last the rest of the day. For the remainder of the morning we took turns watching the fire and preparing lunch.

Long after the sun had passed its midpoint in the sky, Don Juanito and Ramon turned up, back from a very successful fishing trip where they had also speared an *anuje*, a water animal a bit like an otter. The creature was still jerking and I had to avert my gaze as Pashco threw it on the fire and started ripping out its chard fur. Elsa and I finished preparing a lunch of smoked fish and yucca, and we ate with lots of laughing and joking, all of us excited for the ceremony that evening. After lunch I continued to look after the Ayahuasca fire while Pashco completed gutting and cleaning the otter meat for breakfast the next morning.

The Ayahuasca was ready as the sun was beginning to set, and together Pashco and I poured it into a fresh bottle. The smell reached my nose, and shuddering involuntarily, I almost retched. This was a strong brew, and I wondered what tonight was going to bring. I felt like hugging myself in my excitement to be taking Ayahuasca with Jovino.

The sun sank into the horizon, and Walter, Jovino, Lydia, Pepe, Gordo and the children had still not arrived. I felt myself deflating like a balloon, as I had expected Jovino to arrive early in the afternoon, and despite myself had been waiting like a devoted puppy for him. By the time the sky was turning a deep dark black the Shaman, Ramon, Elsa, Pashco, and I were all sitting in a circle, ready and waiting to take the Ayahuasca. The Shaman suggested we started the ceremony, but I insisted that we waited for Jovino, Walter and the others. A while later, the Shaman began to seem annoyed, the ceremony can take up to six hours, and he wanted to start immediately. He told me he did not think they were coming, and insisted that we begin. I nodded, and with a heavy heart took the first cup. Without consciously knowing it I had wanted to show Jovino my power so that he would fall hopelessly in love with me, and finally commit to our relationship.

I stared into the liquid for what seemed like eternity. Every part of me was resisting, and it took all my effort, courage and strength to drink the cup. The moment the thick, dark brew snaked down my throat I felt like Ayahuasca was punishing me for my pathetic and immature ploy to seduce Jovino. The medicine took affect almost instantaneously, and I was intoxicated to the point of total unawareness of my surroundings. As I lost all sense of reality, I saw many spirits entering the ceremony, especially children. Then the floor turned into huge boa constrictors and my heart started to beat faster as I watched them writhe and squirm around my legs as they entered my body. The Shaman had warned me about these visions, and from my own experiences I knew that serpents are at the heart of the Ayahuasca journey. I felt so unreal and detached that I was emotionless.

From a great distance I heard a commotion going on as Jovino, Walter, Gordo, Lydia, Pepe, Doily and Eric arrived, but I was no longer aware of what was going on around me, or even of who I was. I wasn't in control of either my body or my mind. I was almost totally disconnected from this life, as if I had one foot in our worldly dimension and one foot in another.

Jovino began to vomit and the Shaman ordered me to go over to him and shake the *shacapa*. This could have been my moment to prove myself to him but I was too out of my mind to realise it. I shook the *shacapa* over him but he was like a stranger to me, and I could not relate to him on either a physical or sexual level. I then went over to Walter but I was still too intoxicated to consciously help heal him either. I was not in control like I had been in the previous healing ceremonies we had done. After I had shaken the *shacapa* over Walter I was relieved to be able to return to my place in the circle, where I felt safe.

The Shaman changed his *icaros* and suddenly my body was vomiting violently as though trying to rid itself of something. I retched until I thought my stomach would be turned inside out. My throat burned, my eyes burned, my whole body burned as I tried to shift the blockage that my gut was so desperately trying to eject. At the point where I couldn't physically retch anything more, and tears of pain and frustration were pouring down my face and out of my nose, the Shaman appeared at my side and started to shake the *shacapa* over my head and body. I became conscious of the noise of waterfalls, and felt a huge stirring in my lower belly as the obstacle was released. My mind, in an unconscious state, could not register what it was that I had thrown up and got rid of, but I knew that it had been a major obstruction on my path.

I slid to the floor and a silver ladder appeared leading into the clouds. I began to climb it, until I reached heaven and entered into it. From this place I saw that I could overcome the impasse, and that I was protected and guided. From my inebriated, uncontrolled state I saw my teacher's true healing power, and I was in awe of him, for despite his intoxicated state he did not lose control at all during the ceremony, healing each and every person that needed him. Tirelessly, he sang the *icaros* while holding the energy and leading us all on our own individual vision quests, as well as overseeing my journey as his apprentice. His healing power brought me to my senses and I could see how futile my yearning and desire to be a powerful healer and shaman really was.

Then it was as if the fog lifted, and I saw with clarity my relationship with Jovino. It had all been a distraction from the shaman's path. I had fallen into the same trap as Pepe, the ego trap that so many apprentices are ensnared by. Whereas Pepe had turned to alcohol to satisfy his ego, I had embarked on an affair with Jovino. The part of me that needed to feel human and real was craving affection, a sense of belonging. Jovino, in the moment, had made me feel wanted, needed and loved. My ego had reasserted its position as master of my actions and reactions as my mind had tied itself up in knots. I had forgotten to listen to my heart, as I tried desperately to control and manipulate the situation to suit my own desires and wants, without accepting things as they are.

All my fanciful ideas of healing Jovino and Walter had turned to dust. Why? Because I wanted to heal them to enhance my own self-importance, rather than unconditionally, from my heart. I didn't even know if I loved Jovino. I desired him, yes. But was that real love or just the fulfilment of a need within me? I had to make a serious decision to either start a proper and committed relationship with Jovino, forgetting this path, or complete the apprenticeship with the Shaman.

Before I had time to regain control of myself and assist the Shaman the ceremony was over and the kerosene lamp lit. Nothing had gone the way I had planned it. I came back to my senses and was shocked to see how many people had taken Ayahuasca that night. Bodies were lying all over the place. The Shaman had tirelessly initiated and watched over the ceremony without any help at all from his apprentice.

I was the first to leave the ceremony and staggered to my bed, desperate to be away from everyone, especially Jovino, and feel safe under my *mosquitero*. It had been a disastrous night in terms of my expectations. Instead I had been on a massive journey of self-discovery, and, being so close to understanding the obstacles blocking my path, was now able to decide what I wanted to do. I just needed to put into action everything I had learnt so far.

I awoke the next morning feeling confused but calm. Messages from within were telling me I had to go to the medicinal garden to find the answers to some of my questions, but breakfast was nearly ready, and there was no time to be alone. There were many of us to feed and we all sat in the small *casita* eating fresh otter stew, yucca and plantain. Seeing a space next to Pepe, I sat beside him. It was the first opportunity I'd had to talk with him about his apprenticeship, and his experiences with healing and Ayahuasca. I could see Jovino looking at us from across the room but I was too embarrassed to return the eye contact. My feelings for Jovino had predominantly subsided, partly because of the visions I had experienced the night before, and partly because I was embarrassed by my own hidden agenda. I had thought my feelings for Jovino were genuine, but last night Ayahuasca had shown me the truth, and I was scared that he could see through my lies.

Ignoring Jovino's presence I tried to engage myself in the conversation with Pepe, who was confirming to me that the only way to truly heal was to be without ego. He talked like he was an expert on the subject, but like so many people who give advice he had an intellectual understanding of the way of the shaman, but lacked the ability to actually practice it.

Eventually, breakfast was cleared up and Pepe, Gordo, Jovino, Walter, Lydia and the children made their way back to the village. I was relieved to see them go, as I didn't want it to seem obvious that I was avoiding Jovino. Peace and tranquillity were once again restored, both to myself and to the rainforest.

Ramon, Pashco and the Shaman went to the small chakra to inspect the vegetables, Elsa and her family were washing clothes and preparing lunch, and I had the time to escape to our medicinal garden, just as the message had been telling me to.

Since I had first seen the spirits, who exist regardless of whether we believe in them or not, the veil separating our dimension and theirs had been getting thinner. Ayahuasca was finely tuning my sixth sense, and though I was also starting to hear the spirits without the Ayahuasca I still could not see them. In *El Centro*, however, I was able to connect with them much more easily then I could in the village, especially in the medicinal garden the Shaman had created. These spirits, many of whom were children, would commune with me, to guide and help me understand some of what was happening to me.

Sitting on a log I breathed in the clear, clean scent of the forest and stilled my mind. I couldn't see them, but I could sense a presence around me and knew they were here to help me.

*"Rebekita, let go of the need to be desired by men. This is a distraction that is not serving you. Concentrate on healing and serving; this is your purpose. You have the potential to be a healer like your teacher, Don Juanito, who is a great healer, but the healing you have been doing is not the healing of the rainforest. It is time for you now to follow the way of the shaman and chupe the disease out of the patient as all the shaman and their apprentices before you have done."* They said.

*"Rebekita, to really be a healer you must first learn to heal yourself. To heal yourself you must first learn to love yourself, and in order to love yourself you must first 'know' yourself. Only then can you be who you truly are. Only then will you be free to be the healer that every human has the potential to be."* They said.

*An angel is one who shines with universal light, one who provides in the true spirit of love, giving and receiving and bringing happiness to themselves and others."* They said.

As the messages ended, I knew it was time to complete the

apprenticeship and let go of my relationship with Jovino. My heart filled with gratitude and I thanked them for their wisdom. As I made my way back to the *casita* where I was sleeping, a bubble of joy and happiness rose within me. I had made the decision. I was strong enough to overcome the impasse. No more distractions, no more games. Nothing could stop me now. Grabbing my towel I went to the stream to bathe. As I washed away the experience of the night before, I felt a warm glow throughout my body.

* * *

I was impatient to take Ayahuasca again as I could feel that I was close to breaking through, but the Shaman said that we had too much work to do in the *chakra*. He was adamant that we could not continue to take anymore Ayahuasca and cultivate vegetables. He never did say why, but I guessed that it interfered with the energy of the plants. It was decided that we would work in the *chakra* for two days, take Ayahuasca on the full moon, and then return to the village in time for Primavera. I was frustrated with the decision, but I had to trust that the Shaman knew best, and not hurry a process I could not fully understand.

At last, I was beginning to really see how pointless it was to worry about what might or might not happen in a future that is always in motion, so that evening, as we finished the otter stew, I handed Don Juanito forty soles. I knew it was going to leave me short, but it felt better to give the money to Doily, and see the joy on her face as her dream of being the *Primavera Queen* came one step closer.

The next morning the Shaman suggested we go for one of our long walks in the rainforest, and I was surprised to see Ramon joining us. He stared at me, looking like a Rambo of the Amazon, with his bare chest of raw muscle and sinew, the shotgun slung across his back and a machete in his hand. I looked questioningly at the Shaman and he told me that Ramon was going to hunt some food for us.

Usually I always felt so peaceful and happy as we plunged into the deep green, but this time I had some foreboding without knowing why. Something in Ramon's eyes had scared me. I also felt separate from the Shaman, as if he was far away from me. I sensed some kind of danger and a shiver of fear went up and down my spine, but nothing seemed obvious. It was as if the rainforest no longer vibrated with healing green energy, but was instead dangerous and dark. As Ramon walked off into the jungle to follow the footprints of the *majass*, the Shaman and I continued on our way. I felt a sigh of relief as the *selva* returned to the peaceful, healing place I had always known it to be.

The Shaman and I sat on a log sharing a cigarette.

"So, my little *shamana*," he said, "you are growing very quickly, and you are healing already."

"You really think so?" I asked, surprised. This was the first time the Shaman had mentioned anything about my progress to me.

The Shaman looked at me with a serious eye. "Of course, I have seen your body, mind and soul, and it is much cleaner now. Now it is time to start healing with *chuping*. You have seen me do this many times. I place my lips over the sick area and create a vacuum to suck out the sickness. Tomorrow night we will take Ayahuausca again and you will heal Elsa with this technique."

"But Shaman, how does *chuping* cure the patient?" I asked.

"Rebekita, do not get attached to the form. *Chuping* does not cure the patient. The healing power is in the intention of the healer and the patient, whatever form the healing takes," he answered.

"But I am still unsure of exactly how the Ayahuasca assists the Shaman. What is it that makes Her so powerful?" I asked.

"No one knows how it works, but something happens to the shaman when Ayahuasca is taken consistently, and over a period of time. We believe the cells within the body change. Ayahuasca has the magical power to wrap itself around each cell, becoming a part of them. Once the medicine becomes one with you, the doorway is open, and the shaman can understand other people's intentions, thoughts and purposes. This helps the shaman heal even when the patient does not know what is wrong with them. But this process takes time, because the cells have to reach a certain level of purification before the Ayahuasca can merge with them. This is signified in our visions as serpents spiralling around each other."

If my cells were facing their truth as well maybe every part of me was awakening. Body, mind and spirit, I thought.

"How does an *Ayahausquero* know when this has happened?" I enquired.

"The shaman knows because his life will never be the same again," Don Juanito answered mysteriously. I felt an urge to have this experience, but I pushed it away, knowing that yearning for it would probably be just another barrier to actually experiencing it.

The sound of a gun shot, and then another, in the distance broke our conversation. "Come, Ramon has caught our supper," shouted the Shaman as he leapt off the log. Quickly we walked towards the sound of the gunfire as birds and monkeys squawked and shrieked overhead, reacting to the harsh sound that had disturbed the natural rhythm of the rainforest. We soon found Ramon tying two toucans together. I looked on horrified. I had only seen these exotic birds in zoos, not as my supper. Sometimes I still found it hard to accept the killing of beautiful birds like the toucan for food. He had not found *majass*, but had killed a large rat instead. That afternoon we all sat around eating toucan soup. The rat soup, which I was told was delicious, I couldn't bring myself to even try.

The next night the Shaman, Elsa, Ramon and I sat in the Ayahuasca ceremony. The Shaman passed me the first cup; this time the fear had gone and in its place was a deep respect for this medicine. I stared into the mysterious red brown liquid, thanking Her for all she had shown me, as gratitude for the healing and the visions I had experienced poured from my heart. I gulped down the Ayahuasca, feeling it rich and drinkable again as it snaked down my throat. The cup was passed around, and then the Shaman gave me the *shacapa*. After a while he blew out the kerosene lamp and started chanting. Very soon I was in the tunnel of the snake and yet I was also aware of shaking the *shacapa*, and could follow the words and sounds of the *icaros* the Shaman was chanting.

We were all intoxicated, but I felt some degree of control, and then the Shaman pointed at Elsa. I went over and shook the *shacapa* over her head and body. She was very intoxicated and obviously suffering. I was aware of the healing spirits surrounding us and helping me with the process. I tried to feel her pain in my body, and felt a shooting pain in my stomach. I lifted up her t-shirt and placed my lips over the area where I could feel the pain in my own body. I then created a vortex of energy around the area with my lips as though I was drawing something out like a vacuum cleaner, and spat it out. The bile rose immediately, and I vomited hard over the side of the balcony. As I sat back down I was aware that something within me had gone, been vomited up, and had left the space and light needed to allow me to heal using this technique. I *chuped* Elsa's stomach a number of times until I could no longer feel the pain in my own body, and completed the healing by shaking the *shacapa* over her head and body. I then lit my pipe and breathed smoke over her, at which point she vomited for some time.

I went back to my spot near the Shaman, and he asked me to *chupe* his right arm that had been bothering him for a few years but had started to get worse. I continued healing my teacher and shaking the *shacapa* for the rest of the ceremony. I was attentive throughout, despite my own intoxication, and I could sense the spirits assisting me. I felt the potent flow of healing energy, and suddenly comprehended the importance of the apprenticeship I had undertaken. For the first time I actually felt that I was part of this ancient healing tradition.

Later that night when everyone was asleep I felt restless, and went to sit on the bench in the courtyard. As I watched a huge storm rage in the distant sky I was reminded of the storm I had encountered in Machu Picchu. I had felt so separated then, so afraid and alone. I was learning that being alone was only a state of mind. In reality, at every moment, we are connected to the source, to nature, to creation, to our higher selves, and this connection is experienced through love.

As the countless stars twinkled in the deep black of the sky above my head, I realised that everything was just energy and matter constantly changing and flowing, a river of life.

When had humans decided to try to control this organic, evolving life force? When had humans decided to fight against the natural rhythms of life, placing our faith and trust in the man-made, dogmatic rules and regulations that keep us trapped in fear and guilt? Why were so many world leaders corrupt and greedy, and why were there so few beacons of light in the political arena? Or maybe it had always been like this, and humans were reaching the climactic point in their evolution. Maybe it was just time for change and a new beginning, a new way of living. Looking around me I wondered whether life was only as real as a page from a storybook. Perhaps it was time to write new myths, philosophies and ideas based on different values such as Love, Harmony, Integrity, and Respect.

I did not have the answers, but as I watched the stars and planets whirling above me far away in the huge universe, I knew that I was a part of this great mysterious thing called life. The only change I could make was within myself. I had to start with myself and let that spread as a tiny ripple outwards to the rest of the world.

## CHAPTER TWELVE

## *Shattered Images*

*The tidal wave was almost upon us. I was in a canoe with my mother and my sister. They were very frightened, but I reassured them, trusting that 'Dios es Grande.' There was no fear when the tidal wave came and we were pulled under the water. We could still breathe, and I realised I really was protected and loved. If death came it was time for me to die. And then I awoke.*

The next morning I woke up chanting 'heal and serve,' and could still feel the healing energy course through my body. I had broken through the impasse and a powerful change was happening within me. My doubt and confusion had dissolved and I was ready to take on the next stage of the apprenticeship with renewed vigour and energy.

After breakfast we left *El Centro* and returned to the village. That afternoon, as we settled back into our normal routine, I felt a quiet and peaceful calm descend over our little *casita* by the river. Jovino had gone to Iquitos, Ramon was fishing, the Shaman rested, Pashco was in the *chakra*, and Elsa and Esther were visiting their mother in the village. I knew this was only a reflection of my own sense of wellbeing. Previously, I would have panicked about being left alone, especially after an Ayahuasca ceremony. I now welcomed the opportunity to have this time and space, in order to integrate a little of what I was experiencing, and listen to the voice within that was now louder than ever.

Walking alone in the forest without the Shaman felt unreal, as though I was in the world of dreams, and had been there before in another age. There was nothing to think about because everything was happening perfectly and in harmony with the heart. Worrying or reminiscing was not going to change reality at that moment. Rebekita was walking in the ancient Amazon, and she was happy, truly happy. Not because of any external stimuli, not because she was with a man, but because she was beginning to accept herself as she was.

Sitting by a little spot overlooking the river that the Shaman and I had visited a few times on our walks, I let the sound of the water lull me into a meditative state as it flowed toward the great Amazon. Gazing into the river I wondered if it was possible to actually experience it, to merge with it, to become one with it, and then I remembered it was all happening perfectly. If it was, the experience would come at the right time.

That evening Pashco and the Shaman were in a playful mood, and asked me if I would like to stay and live with them in the rainforest as their adopted daughter. Immediately, they began planning my marriage. Soon we were roaring with laughter as they imagined me married to various single men living in the village. I smiled inwardly when they did not mention Jovino's name, but lacked the courage to add it to the list. However, in their jest there was an element of seriousness, and they offered to build me a *casita* with a *chakra* and my own medicine garden. We agreed we would bring Westerners here to take Ayahuasca. It sounded perfect and idyllic and I would be able to heal and be who I was, free from the limited perceptions of Western society.

The conversation affected me, and later that night as I looked out over the river, the night sky glistening with diamond stars, confusion clouded my mind. My year in Peru was nearly up, and soon I had to decide whether to stay here or use my return flight home. It was a hard decision. I had never been so happy and contented. This felt more like home then London ever had. But somehow I knew that despite my deep connection with this magical place, my destiny was in the West.

As I sat in the silence, I heard the voice within tell me that I needed to bring the Shaman's message back to the West. To spread the wisdom and insight I had learnt from this special place and to share the experiences I had encountered. "What do I need to do back in the West," I whispered to the night sky. "Just be yourself, Rebekita and trust. Be patient, the path will show itself," was the answer.

The next morning after breakfast the Shaman and I went for a walk. He took me to a beautiful part of the rainforest that we had not been to before, pulsating with energy and vitality. Deep in the rainforest the Shaman turned and asked me if I was serious about staying with him in the Amazon. I wanted to talk to him about the messages I had heard the night before but before I could answer he leaned toward me and, with lust in his eyes, tried to kiss me. I was surprised, sickened, angry and disappointed all at the same time and looked away embarrassed. He told me that if I slept with him his semen would make me more powerful. I looked at Don Juanito in disgust. That was the philosophy of many gurus and shaman, but I hadn't expected it from my teacher. Racking my brains I tried to understand what had changed, but I could find nothing in my behaviour that might have given a sexual message to the Shaman. Diplomatically, I explained that I saw him as a father, and could not embark on a physical relationship.

"You will never stay in the rainforest anyway, your destiny is in the West where you belong," the Shaman said angrily as he got up from the log, and without looking at me stormed into the rainforest. I ran to catch up with him, and could feel his anger with me as we walked through the lush foliage in silence. I felt angry too, because as my teacher he should have known better. I was disappointed that he thought I would actually have sex with him. It also put me in an awkward position, for Don Juanito still did not know that I had been in a relationship with his son.

Struggling with my confusion, I remembered to breathe and tried to focus on the moment. I soon felt the emotional charge surrounding the incident dissolve and I started to feel blissfully happy again. Life is easy when I was not wallowing in other people's reactions towards me.

When we arrived back at the *casita*, Pashco immediately knew something was wrong, but nothing was said. She had prepared lunch and we all sat down in stony silence. The Shaman did not look or speak to me, and neither did Pashco. Without asking what had happened, Pashco had automatically sided with the Shaman. I would always be an outsider, and a feeling of sadness descended on me as we ate, the camaraderie of the previous night forgotten.

While I was sitting in the hammock, resting after lunch and writing my diary, the Shaman came over and told me that he had a lot of work to do in the *chakras* and that we would not be taking Ayahuasca as planned. As he was telling me this I started boiling. My immediate reaction was to terminate the apprenticeship and go straight to Iquitos on the next boat. It was a form of blackmail showing me that I could have had it all if I had slept with him. Then clarity hit and I stopped reacting. I no longer had to spend my life trying to appease people and make them happy. I only had the power to make myself happy, and I wasn't going to have sex with the Shaman regardless of the consequences. This was my test to stick to my principles, to follow my truth and not feel guilty for Don Juanito because I could not fulfil his needs. Though I was fearful of the reaction of the Shaman, I knew I could not go against myself now.

Still feeling confused I wandered to the river's edge where I could hear the voice within. As I sat there feeling the heat of the sun on my face, my mind slowly fell into silence, and I understood that I was disappointed with the Shaman. But he had not changed. He was still being who he was. It was I who had to change my perception of him. He was a remarkable shaman and healer, but he was also just another fragile and vulnerable human being. I had put him on a spiritual pedestal, and was now finding it difficult to accept that he was not as infallible as I wanted him to be. Even this powerful shaman could be controlled by his ego.

It began to be clear that I was only really seeing what I wanted to see with all the people I interacted with. I rarely ever saw them for who they truly were. All the people in my life were only reflections of who I was, a figment of my imagination, of my thought patterns, of my conditioning. I was closer to understanding the concept of unconditional love. As my own mask was melting I was able to see other people for who they truly were, and not who I thought or wanted them to be, regardless of how they acted towards me.

The next night, the conversation the day before forgotten, we had the Ayahuasca ceremony as planned, but the Shaman only took *Agua de Florida* because he claimed he wanted to work in the *chakra* the next morning. I didn't believe him, and sensed he was doing it to continue punishing me for not having sex with him. That night Elsa and I took Ayahuasca. The Shaman chanted for about an hour, and then he started to speak to Elsa about how bad I was to him, and how I made everyone feel special and wanted and loved, except him.

I was only in control of my own emotional responses, and instead of feeling angry and hurt I sent love to the Shaman and Elsa, and in return felt a warm flow of peace and harmony throughout my body. As I *chuped* Elsa the love vibrated through me, and the healing energy seemed more intense and effective.

Next morning my head and body ached, and I was really looking forward to my walk in the rainforest with the Shaman, wanting to reconnect with him. After breakfast I went to collect water from the river, and when I returned Pashco told me that

Don Juanito and Ramon had left to go hunting *anuje*. I couldn't believe that they had gone without me, but then an interesting thing happened. Instead of getting upset and being consumed with negative thoughts, I just let it go and tried to see the opportunity that had suddenly presented itself. Pashco must have felt sorry for me because a bit later, as I was swinging in the hammock, she unexpectedly asked me if I would like to work with her in the *chakra*. It was a wonderful opportunity to spend some time with her, and maybe get to know her better. About an hour later, as we were inspecting the vegetables and yucca, Jovino appeared unannounced.

My heart gave a leap of joy to have this time with him without the Shaman interfering, and again my heart gave a prayer of thanks that I had not gone hunting. Since the Ayahuasca ceremony at *El Centro* the passion between Jovino and I had been extinguished. Having seen that my lust for Jovino was really my ego needing to satiate itself, I knew that there could be nothing more between us. Simultaneously, Jovino had come to the same conclusion. He was about to become engaged to a woman in Iquitos, and I had been a distraction for him too as he fought with the responsibility of marriage.

Neither of us needed to explain what was happening. Our connection was deep enough for us to understand it on a soul level, and now we had our friendship back. It was wonderful talking with Jovino again about what was happening to me. He understood the situation with his father, and told me it was Don Juanito's *manera* when he couldn't get what he wanted. By talking things became much clearer, and I stopped taking it all so personally. That afternoon the Shaman and Ramon returned carrying an *anuje* between them. Don Juanito had cheered up, and the energy seemed much brighter and lighter, or maybe that was because I was much happier myself.

That evening as I was preparing for bed, a tremendous pain ripped through my head like an explosion, and continued through my body. Losing all sense of balance I collapsed to the floor, crying out in agony as I began to retch. I thought I was going to die. The Shaman heard me and came immediately. He *chuped* my head and then bathed me in *El Camphor* while chanting some *icaros* and I felt as if a wave of pure love flowed between us. The pain subsided and I slept peacefully.

The next morning I awoke bright and early, and everything seemed back to normal. I wasn't sure if Jovino had talked to the Shaman, but at breakfast we agreed to take Ayahuasca that night. This time the Shaman apologised, but said he would only take *El Camphor* because his arm was paining him and he did not have the strength to take Ayahuasca. I knew that this time the Shaman was not punishing me. Over time he had been looking old and exhausted, and his right arm was getting worse. I accepted it, despite my disappointment with the decision.

As we walked to the *chakras* Don Juanito asked me who I was having an affair with, and before I could answer he told me that he knew it was Jovino, his *hijo*. I didn't deny it, instead I looked at my teacher in surprise that he had not confronted me before. The Shaman said he had seen it a long time ago in an Ayahuasca vision, but had said nothing. In his wisdom he had known that I needed to go through the experience for my growth, despite his own needs. The reason why he thought I was so bad to him was because I wouldn't sleep with him, as well as Jovino, because he was the Shaman. Teacher and pupil, pupil and teacher had been guided to learn from each other, consciously and unconsciously, and we laughed because the Shaman knew that the ego lessons were for him too.

The day was spent planting yucca, and as I sowed scenes from my life flashed in my mind. I could see that I was creating everything that happened in my life, based on who I chose to be. My mind then judged everything according to the conditioning and beliefs of that person I had chosen to be. What are right and wrong, failure and success, good and bad, fat and thin, stupid and intelligent, but judgements that only have significance for the individual that makes them? This was truly living a life of suffering, as I tried desperately to manipulate external events to work out in my favour, without knowing what I truly wanted.

After I had experienced the vision of the Shaman in Machu Picchu the flow of life took its course, and led me, by events that seemed out of my control, to where I needed to be. It was my human conditioning that had judged the situation at the hotel, and I had exhausted precious energy trying to fight the flow of life that was leading me to my destiny.

That night, just before we started the Ayahuasca ceremony, the Shaman dropped the bottle of *El Camphor*, smashing it on the floor. Looking at me sheepishly he laughed, and we both knew he had to take Ayahuasca as well. That evening after the sky had become blue-black, and the stars were clear and sparkling, a new moon slowly made her descent into the West. Once again, Don Juanito and I sat opposite each other, ready to take the brew. Just the two of us together, the Shaman and his apprentice.

Taking the Ayahuasca from him I gulped it down. It was strong and powerful as the brew coursed down my throat and into my stomach, as if Ayahuasca knew this would be one of the last times I would take it with the Shaman, and She wanted to show me as much as She could before I returned to the West. The Shaman watched, then smiled. *"Buen Fuerte, Rebekita, Buen Fuerte,"* he said after drinking his cup. He blew out the kerosene lamp, and in the darkness I was surprised to see just how many wise old spirits had come to join us and were watching the ceremony with interest.

I was immediately intoxicated. I tried to shake the *shacapa*, but could not communicate the reflex to my wrist. Weird animals and huge snakes entered my body. My heart started to beat very fast as I became paralysed, and began to vomit, knowing it was the fear of fear itself. Slumping to the ground I tried to catch my breath, but my throat was locked. I gasped for breath. I could not breathe. I was suffering. I was dying. I was alone. Even the Shaman could not help me now. My body was trembling uncontrollably as Death came to sit at my shoulder. Once again, I had come face to face with my mortality. I was going to die. And then I remembered that I had the choice. This time I was ready. I was dying at every moment, but every moment I was closer to death, I was *alive*. As I breathed into the fear of death, accepting it and letting it go, the gateway to consciousness, unique to each and every human being, opened up within me.

The mask disintegrated and I could see. The only fear that existed was the fear I had for myself. For this person called Rebekita. And this fear was the very barrier that stopped me from loving myself. I could blame my suffering on society, religion, my parents, my friends, my lovers and all the other obstructions and limitations I had constructed for myself, but the truth was I did not love myself because I feared who I truly was. This time there was no escape, no distraction, no noise. I was ready to face my fear. To face who I truly was, and accept her with love.

I sat upright like the Shaman had taught me, and I stared straight back at myself. Then, in accordance with the flow of life the fear began to dissolve, and the huge boundless energies of love that had been buried under the fear were freed, leaving a glow of white light that coursed through my body.

The room disappeared as I crossed the threshold into the Void. In the blackness I saw Jesus bathed in silvery moonlight, towering above me on a cross. He looked down on me with infinite love and compassion. "This is my true message," the vision said. "Serve all with unconditional love. Let go of religions that no longer teach truth. The only truth that exists is Love. There is nothing else. When you love yourself everything becomes love, for everything is only a mirror of your thoughts, actions and deeds. To live a life in compassionate love is to live a life in bliss and to become a pure channel for the Christ energy."

Seeing Jesus on the cross, I knew that he was the potential that all human beings can reach. He was not special or chosen but a human that had learnt to live through his heart in unity with everything around him, no longer separated by his ego. Then the sky opened and I saw his spirit go straight to heaven, and as he looked down on me I heard him say, "Let go of ego and live a life of blissful happiness. It is every human's birthright. I am the Way, follow the path of love and you will find salvation."

As the vision faded and the heavens closed I was drifting in space, among the stars and planets that make up this great and glorious universe. I could feel the power and energy of matter when it exists in harmony, and then my body, mind and soul merged with this matter and I became one with it. For a few timeless seconds I became the universe.

Then the Ayahuasca spoke.

*"Rebekita, the dense physical structure that we call the body is only the framework for the soul; in order to experience life as a human you have the mind/ego. Over time this servant has become the master, creating the illusion that the 'I' really exists. Creating the impression of separation."*

*"Can I really reach the same stage as Jesus the Christ?"* I whispered

*"Rebekita, every human has the potential to reach the same stage as Jesus, for everyone, without exception, is part of the universal energy, or as you would say, 'a child of God.' Jesus was liberated because he let go of the perceptions that had kept him 'separate.' He realised he was part of the 'whole.' By liberating himself from ego he no longer feared himself. He had let go of all his limitations and was one with the Creator at every moment. He was a pure channel for the Christ energy."*

*"If love is glowing from the inside it spreads out and touches all those who come into contact with it, like the ripples of a small stone thrown into a pool of water. The more you love the more love there*

*is."*

As I entered the serpent's head through its mouth I became young and innocent again, like a child that trusts and has an unquestioning faith in the wonder of everything. I found myself swooping through the body of this gigantic serpent until I flew out of the tail and into space, experiencing our tiny planet in this massive universe. And I was just one being in a huge universe, one being among billions of beings reincarnating on this planet to play and explore and express who they truly are.

The visions and messages ended and I was back in the ceremony. I became aware of lots of spirit children with us. I leaned over and shook the *shacapa* over the Shaman's arm, head and body, and then a spirit without a head came over to me and instructed me on how to heal the Shaman. The spirit told me that the Shaman was being attacked by a *brujo* that was angry with him for healing Elsa, and for teaching me, a Westerner. It wanted to suck the power out of the Shaman, so he was transferring as much of his wisdom, power and knowledge as he could to me. This, on top of the protection he was giving me from the *brujos*, was making him weak and sick.

Believing the truth of this, my heart overflowed with love and compassion for the sacrifice my teacher was making to preserve this ancient wisdom. I wondered what would happen when I returned to the West. I *chuped* the Shaman's arm, using *Agua de Florida*, which can sometimes intensify the healing process, but this time I knew that it was up to the grace of the healing energies. I could only be the conduit, and send him love and compassion.

As I sat back down I saw a powerful vision of the Ayahuasca vine, and it filled my whole being. My body became heavy as Ayahuasca coursed through it, pumped by my excited heart, connecting to every individual cell. I wondered if my body had reached its 'comfort' stage, remembering what the Shaman had told me about Ayahuasca and its ability to communicate on a cellular level.

When the Shaman lit the lamp the Ayahuasca was still running through my veins, my body still heavy, as though a huge weight was pinning it down. I turned to the Shaman and he looked old and frail. His face was pale and drawn, and the power that he had shown me at the beginning of the apprenticeship was no longer there. He had now passed it on to me. Rebekita had merged with the river. Turning to the Shaman, I filled my pipe and blew it around his head and body as he had done for me on my first Ayahuasca journey.

Gone was the look of lust and control from his eyes, and instead there was respect and admiration for his apprentice, who in her own right had overseen the Ayahuasca ceremony and had almost completed her apprenticeship. Together we sat in silence, love flowing between us. The Shaman and his apprentice, both aware of the enormity of the journey we had taken together, and of how this would change our lives for ever.

## CHAPTER THIRTEEN

## *From Wawita to Amoracita*

*I was lying naked and entwined with another woman in loving and compassionate oneness. The other woman was my self. I had learned to start loving myself, no longer controlled by an illusory image. I was free.*

Early the next morning while we were having breakfast, the Shaman told me that if I left him he would die. He had lost the feeling in his right arm, was in terrible pain, and fearful that there would be no one who could protect him from the *brujos*. Last night, after the ceremony, he had been attacked by a *brujo* who, in the dream world, had pushed him into a deep hole. Calling for help, only I and another Shaman from Santa Clara had come to rescue and protect him. Pepe and the other apprentices had not come to assist him, and now he knew, without doubt, I was his last apprentice. I didn't know what to say. We both knew I had to return to the West, that it was my destiny. The Shaman himself had known that all along. I couldn't stay here and protect him, and yet how could I leave him? And then I remembered that I had to trust in the process, take each moment as it comes, and not worry about the future until I reached it.

Soon after breakfast we made the journey to the *casitas* in *El Centro* to find Ayahuasca, and prepare a fresh batch for me to take to England. We had decided that because the Shaman was very weak and in pain, we would not stay the night in the remote *casitas* in case he took a turn for the worse, but would return to the village before sunset. It was going to be a long day and I had difficulty in motivating my body for the journey, as it still felt really heavy, yet strangely light and airy at the same time. I was excited to be going back to *El Centro*. It was the perfect opportunity to say goodbye to the spirits in my little medicinal garden that had guided me along the way.

We took the small canoe, with Pashco and I doing most of the paddling as the Shaman was unable to use his arm. The walk through the rainforest was relaxing and, because there was no baggage to carry, I was really able to appreciate the beauty of the ancient trees and their foliage. When we arrived at *El Centro* the Shaman went to the *chakra* to look them over, and cut some pineapple. This time it was Pashco and I who went into the rainforest to cut the Ayahuasca.

My mind was tranquil and quiet as we walked to a beautiful part of the rainforest I had never been to before. The sunlight was pouring through the gaps in the trees, power was in the air, and I could feel myself pulsating and vibrating with the glowing vitality and energy of the rainforest. I was connecting with the rhythm of nature, and this time I was honoured to be with a true Shamana, searching for Ayahuasca that she had planted there a long time before.

Pashco and I had experienced a strange relationship; sometimes she treated me as her daughter, and at other times she ignored me, and I felt that she was angry with me for taking Don Juanito from her. Another obstacle to cultivating our relationship was the Shaman. He was very possessive of me, so I'd never really had the chance to get to know her, and she had never opened the door wide enough to let me into her world. But that afternoon I saw her power.

While we were cutting the thick Ayahuasca liana I told her that there had never been anything sexual between the Shaman and me, not a hug, a kiss, nothing. It felt so good telling her that. Looking me in the eye, she said, *"Gracias,"* and I felt a companionship with Pashco that we had not shared before. We spent the afternoon bonding and laughing, two women connected to the Shaman, joined by a destiny that had brought us together.

She told me she was worried about Don Juanito, that she had never seen him this weak before, and that only I could heal him. She agreed with the Shaman that if I left he would die. She asked me to stay with them in the rainforest and offered to help me grow a *chakra* and vegetable garden, and together we would heal. She spoke with a sincerity that bought tears to my eyes, as I realised I had been waiting all this time for her to tell me this. To show me she too supported and understood my apprenticeship. Hearing these words filled my heart with love and pain because I knew it was too late. I could not stay.

Together we sat and chanted the *icaros* to thank the Ayahuasca spirits for their gifts. The feminine power flowed through us, powerful and potent. The Goddess energy was emerging from her cocoon, a butterfly, to spread love.

When we walked back it began to rain hard, sheets of water pouring down out of nowhere, and as we tried to shelter under some trees I saw the spirits of the jungle and heard them singing. I had often felt them, but had never seen or heard them except during the Ayahuasca ceremonies. I was connecting with the magic of the *selva* and it was a mystical experience. The rain cloud soon passed and we made our way back to the *casita*. Pashco went to find the Shaman while I went to my little medicine garden to say goodbye. As soon as I was sitting on my log the spirits were ready and waiting to give me my last message.

*"Rebekita, at every moment you are choosing a new possibility. With every decision we make we are BEING who we choose to be. Love is the only right action. Choose love at every moment, and live in freedom. Nurture your inner voice, your heart, until you make it*

*strong.*

    *Life is just the process of* **Separation**, **Exploration** *and* **Reunion**.*"*

I thanked them for their wisdom, their guidance and their compassionate love for my journey. I did not know when I would return, but I knew that they would always be with me.

Late that afternoon, after eating fresh pineapple and collecting some yucca from the *chakra*, we made our way back home. The next day would be my last in the Amazon, and in the morning Pashco and I were to prepare the Ayahuasca, and then take it with the Shaman on my last night. As we paddled back on the river the sun was setting over the rainforest, turning the sky pink. I let out a long sigh. I had no idea how I felt about leaving.

A part of me was so excited to be going home. The apprenticeship was coming to an end and I was ready to leave. I was looking forward to seeing my parents, my family, Harry and my friends, to speaking English again, and to see just how much I had learnt and how much I had changed. At the same time I was devastated to be leaving the Amazon. This had become my home. I was myself here, happy and contented, and I wondered if I was ever going to find that peace of mind back in the West. Despite feeling that it was my destiny to go back, I took comfort in the thought that if it all went wrong I could always come back to live in the rainforest.

\* \* \*

I awoke at dawn, early enough to experience another peaceful, still morning on the river. The sun was just beginning to appear, and clouds floated across the sky like soft and gentle whispers. Pashco had already begun preparing the Ayahuasca and I went to take over from her. Soon we had beaten all the pieces, and putting them in the cauldron I added tobacco smoke from my pipe. We both added our energy and saliva to the *Vine of the Soul*, and Pashco filled the cauldron with water that she had collected from the river, placing it on the roaring fire. Don Juanito joined us for breakfast. He was still suffering, and had decided to buy some Western medicine for the pain. I was surprised that Don Juanito was resorting to pharmaceuticals. It was an important message that shamanism and conventional medicine can work alongside each other. It is necessary to integrate both in order to heal and prevent disease. While Pashco and the Shaman were gone to buy the medicine in a bigger village further down the river, I lay in the hammock, listening to *Shakira's "Estoy Aqui"* on the cassette player, and watched over the fire.

It seemed a lifetime ago that I was listening to that song in *El Centro*, full of fear, doubt and suffering. That young girl no longer existed. She had leapt into the fire and had emerged cleansed and purified. By following her heart and completing the apprenticeship, she had made it, fulfilled her destiny and made her dream come true. Life would never be the same again.

A few hours later Don Juanito returned, and we went for a final walk to the village to say goodbye to some of the people I had made friends with, while Pashco continued to tend the Ayahuasca fire. I expected our last day to be full of laughter and reminiscing, but it was quite the opposite. Instead, it was an emotionally painful afternoon, with the Shaman being facetious and stubborn. My heart was heavy as I sensed that Don Juanito was in turmoil at my leaving, and I did not know what to say to him. I wanted to shake him, to make him see that we were wasting valuable time, but he didn't seem to care. Throughout the afternoon the gulf between us seemed to get bigger as he became more distant and unapproachable.

Later that afternoon, the Ayahuasca had been decanted ready for drinking that evening, and I had come back from saying goodbye to my special places in the Amazon. The Shaman and I were sitting on the steps, watching the sun make its descent into the river. As we smoked our pipes together the familiar energy was back. I immortalised the picture of sitting beside my teacher as the sky turned pink, orange and purple, and a flock of colourful parrots screeched and cawed overhead, flying on a wind moist with the coming rains.

Turning, the Shaman looked deep into my eyes, just as he had done the first time we met. He was seeing beyond the physical and into my soul. In a voice filled with love and respect and wisdom he said to me "Rebekita, you are no longer my *linda wawita*. You are now an *Amoracita,*"

The words needed no explanation as they touched my heart, filling my eyes with tears. *Amoracita* is taken from the word *amor* and means one that has learnt to love themselves. By honouring me with this title, he saw me as more than a healer. Calling me an *amoracita*, he had recognised that by learning to love myself I had healed myself, and by healing myself I was on the path to being able to heal others. This was the greatest compliment he could have given me and I had no words to offer in return. No words could do his praise justice. In that moment I knew I was no longer the apprentice.

We had fulfilled our destiny, the Shaman and I, and I did not know whether I would see him again in this earthly body. There was a pain in my heart that was so tender. I loved this man beyond words, and he loved me exactly the same. We were two beings that had been brought together this lifetime to fulfil our karma. I was so honoured and grateful and humbled for the experience. I took his hand in mine and kissed it, and he placed his other hand over my head in blessing, and we sat there sending out thanks and love in silence.

As darkness came Walter, Lydia, Eric and Doily came to say goodbye with presents and gifts they had made. I was overwhelmed by the love and respect they had for me, and the way they had accepted me into their hearts and their family. We sat around talking and laughing, remembering some of the funny stories and incidents that had happened over the months I had been in the rainforest. Throughout the visit the Shaman had become withdrawn, and would not join us or engage in the conversation.

As the night got blacker I asked the Shaman when the Ayahuasca ceremony would begin. He said he could no longer lead the ceremony because he was now taking Western medication. Walter saw the look in my eye and said he wouldn't mind drinking. I turned to Pashco who agreed to take the ceremony with me. A few minutes later we were sitting in a circle, and it was Pashco who handed me the first cup. Staring into the deep brown liquid of the fresh brew for the last time, gratitude poured from every cell in my body as I thanked Ayahuasca for everything I had seen and experienced in the ceremonies. I drank the rich, bitter, thick liquid and it snaked down my throat. After Walter and Pashco had drunk their cups, Pashco blew out the kerosene lamp and began to sing *icaros* in her own language. The visions took on a power and a vividness that left me in no doubt that they were real.

As Pashco sang her songs the Goddess within me began to stir. My body became heavy and I was completely intoxicated. I could feel the strangest sensation as the Ayahuasca began to communicate with each cell, entwining with it, transmuting it, and becoming a part of it. My body seemed to glow from the inside and experience the truth; that we are all matter and energy with no form, no beginning, and no end. We are all connected to the same source. There is no separation.

Everything is in constant flow, in constant motion. In its purest vibratory form I was divine energy. There is only one law on this planet, the law of nature; the more we love, the more love we receive, the more we fear, the more fear we receive, the more we hate, the more hate we receive.

What the Shaman had said had been right after all, Ayahuasca does become merged with the lifeforce and the DNA, because I could feel it happening in my own body. I couldn't move or sit comfortably; the only position that I could bear was slouching forward. My body was flowing with golden white light as the Ayahuasca transferred its final messages of wisdom and knowledge through my being, the energy and matter that make up this physical body. For the rest of my life I would be bound to Ayahuasca, and She to me.

I took over some of the ceremony, singing my *icaros* in English and shaking the *shacapa*. We both did some healing on Walter and Don Juanito, and then Pashco did some healing on me, and I on her. Throughout the ceremony I felt the flow of Goddess energy reaching far into the cosmos. Ayahuasca, Pashco and I, it was the reawakening of feminine energy that is not only holistic, but also unconditional, nurturing and empowering, and desperately needed on the planet in order to redress the current imbalance.

Pashco lit the kerosene lamp and its orange glow illuminated the room. The Shaman had already gone to bed, and I knew that this ceremony had completed my apprenticeship. The Shaman's last apprentice was no longer the girl who was addicted to her sufferings. Those sufferings that had stopped her from being who she truly was. She was now a free woman, a shaman, and it was time she walked with head upright and eyes open, ready to live in joy and happiness.

* * *

The next morning I awoke to a cold and miserable dawn. The rain was pouring in sheets and everything was deathly still. I had hoped for a beautiful sunny day, but instead of reacting with disappointment I interpreted it as the ending of my apprenticeship, this ending of the dry season and the coming of the rains. It was time for change, for new beginnings, heralded by a new season.

Pashco and Don Juanito were still sleeping and I knew something was not right; there was a strange energy in the air. I woke them to start organising our bags for the journey to Iquitos, and went to the river to bathe. My mind was foggy, but my body felt purified and healed, so light and airy. I was at peace.

The final ceremony with Pascho, and the bonding with the feminine energy, was the completion that I needed. Despite my feelings of reservation about leaving the Shaman, I knew I could not stay any longer. After dressing, the Shaman asked me to sit in front of him. He took his pipe and blew smoke all over my head and body, telling me it would make me strong, but his heart did not seem to be in it. I could feel the Goddess energy flowing through me, and I ached to return the blessing, but did not have the courage to offer it. The gulf between us had grown so big that I did not know how to cross it to say goodbye.

The Shaman left to go to meet the boat that would take me to Iquitos, and I prepared myself to leave. Sometime later Walter and Don Juanito came into the *casita*, and Walter asked me how much money I was giving to the Shaman for his services. I offered what the Ayahuasca told me was the right amount. It was as if he had been waiting for this moment, because without warning, Don Juanito went crazy, mad with anger, shouting at me that the money was not enough, and that he expected much more for everything he had done for me.

Before he had even given me time to explain, he decided not to come to Iquitos with me. I stood there in bewilderment, for I knew it wasn't about the money. When I had lost my pouch both he and I had been tested on our commitment to undertake the apprenticeship. I had been tested on my dedication to the path and the Shaman had been tested to ensure that his intentions to teach me were pure, and that he had no expectations of financial reward for the apprenticeship. He would reason with no one, cursing me, the *gringa*, the months we had shared together forgotten in a fit of rage and pain.

As the Shaman blasted me with venom, I felt compassion and love for the teacher that was rejecting me at the moment when I was walking away, maybe never to see him again in an earthly body. Instead of backing down, offering more money, trying to appease him, I let him be who he wanted to be, remaining centred in myself.

This was the final test from the man who had taught me how to love unconditionally. He was showing me that I no longer needed his approval, for I had the strength to walk away with compassionate love in my heart, regardless of his actions towards me. My destiny was calling me to another part of the world, and it was time to leave.

As I boarded the boat the Shaman was nowhere to be seen. I saw Pashco wave from the *casita*, and I waved back as the boat left the bank and made its way down river. "Goodbye, Don Juanito, and thank you, thank you, we will meet again but probably not in our earthly bodies. I love you," I whispered silently as the tears streamed down my face. The boat rounded the bend, and the *casita* was no longer in sight.

As I sat in the boat my heart ached for the Shaman, for the pain I knew he was going through, and for not allowing us to say goodbye. I did not know why he had decided to let me go into the unknown alone. But I did not blame him, or feel angry with him. I was sure he had reasons that would become clear eventually.

As the boat made its way down the river, I was again invited to sit on the roof of the boat and the welcoming breeze blew the cobwebs of the Ayahuasca ceremony from my mind. I was back on the Amazon with its unending horizon vibrating with vitality and life. The rainforest on either side radiating its green hues into the atmosphere. I breathed in the thick, clean air and released a rush of excitement for the future. I was free, really free and liberated. As the Shaman raged I had still been at peace within myself, unaffected by his anger and fury. I didn't need the Shaman to love me or respect me. I still loved him.

As Iquitos came into sight and we neared the port I was nervous. I was about to reconnect with my world, the world of technology and development, chaos and pollution, systems and controls. Time had not sat still for me. I had not been in contact with anyone for months. I wondered whether Harry would still be waiting for me, if my mother, my father, my family and friends were all safe and healthy. If I had been forgotten. I could only wait and see.

Soon I would be on the plane, winging my way to a new life, a new beginning and a new purpose on the other side of the world. I still wasn't sure what I needed to do in the West, but that didn't matter. It was all happening perfectly and I trusted, without doubt, that my heart would lead me to where I needed to be.

However, things had changed. I no longer had the safety of knowing I could escape to the forest if it all fell apart. The apprenticeship was complete and by his anger, Don Juanito had made it clear that the door was now closed for me. It would be difficult to return without his blessing. All I could do was put my intention out into the future, and see what came back. If I was meant to return, I would.

I gave a prayer of thanks to all those beings that I had met on the way who had helped me reach this point in my life. Most importantly, I remembered to thank myself for taking the risk, and leaving everything behind to go into the unknown, to follow my dream. I thanked myself for the courage and the perseverance I had shown during the apprenticeship, and for the discipline of staying when things got really tough. I was remembering who I truly was, a divine being of love, and now all I needed to do was live it.

As we approached Iquitos I could see billows of grey and black smoke pouring out all over the city. The men working on the boat told us that the border dispute between Peru and Ecuador, raging since 1942, had ended that morning with Fujimori, the Peruvian President, handing over the disputed piece of land to Ecuador. In that moment Peruvians were now Ecuadorians. The people of Iquitos had united in retaliation and were rioting. The city was in flames. We docked, and as I watched the chaos and anger unleash itself around me, I saw how it reflected my own journey.

Just as I had to go through the fire of chaos to burn the ego and emerge on the other side transformed, a butterfly, Iquitos was going through it's own trial by fire. The burning of the city demonstrated the anger and helplessness of people who no longer felt in control of their destinies and lives. To me, Iquitos had become a microcosm of the larger antipathy of the people to our political, economic and religious systems. As these systems start to break down we feel as if we are losing our safety, security and our identity, as we fall into chaos. We are forgetting that something new is breaking through and that the caterpillar must die to allow the butterfly to live. So too must the old ways collapse, allowing new ways to emerge.

As the mob raged around me I looked up at the blue of the Amazonian sky and saw the Shaman looking down at me. I heard him say:

"Only Unconditional Love can create a new reality based on harmony."

**"Your destiny and the destiny of every living being is to be who you truly are – divine beings full of love and light. Your purpose, and the purpose of every living being, is to heal and serve and love unconditionally, in your own special and unique way."**

His eyes were twinkling like two pearls in the moonlight, his round face beaming and glowing with the light of love and compassion, blessing and protecting me for the next stage of my journey…

THE BEGINNING

# EPILOGUE

*At no time since my return have I felt the need to return to the rainforest, or to the Shaman and his family. The Shaman had shut the door and has not called me back. Our time together was complete and he had taught me that I no longer needed him. It was time to find the answers from within, with the tools he and the Ayahuasca had imparted. In his infinite wisdom he had taught me how to be unafraid to say goodbye and let go. I had never been so happy in my life as when I was in the jungle, but my image of it as a paradise does not truly exist. I believe that when we follow our dreams a greater force protects us, and throughout my time I did not experience the dangerous or difficult elements of living there. The Shaman had given me the freedom to move on and fulfil my destiny in the West.*

*By facing the fears that had kept me paralysed I learnt, and am still learning, to accept myself and love myself as I truly am.*